Modern Literature of Cambodia:
Transnational Voices of Transformation

Edited and with an Introduction by
Teri Shaffer Yamada

Nou Hach Literary Association: Translation Series

'Just a Human Being' and other Tales from Contemporary Cambodia (2013), Nou Hach Literary Association Translation Series, No. 1.

Modern Literature of Cambodia: Transnational Voices of Transformation (2016), Nou Hach Literary Association Translation Series, No. 2.

The Nou Hach Literary Association (http://nouhachjournal.net) is a non-profit NGO established in 2002 to support writers, literature and literacy in Cambodia. All proceeds from this book are used to support its writers workshops.

Cover art from the painting "Sea Feather" by OEUR Sokuntevy with permission of the artist.

Copyright © 2016 by Teri Shaffer Yamada.
No part of this collection can be reproduced or redistributed in any manner without permission of the editor.

ISBN-13: 978-1517435462
ISBN-10: 1517435463

DEDICATION AND ACKNOWLEDGEMENTS

Modern Literature of Cambodia: Transnational Voices of Transformation is the second volume in the Nou Hach Literary Association's (NHLA) translation series. It aspires to inform a wider audience about new Cambodian literature in both English and English translation in the genres of short fiction, essay, poetry, and drama. It expands the geographical location of authors from Cambodia to the United States and includes works by second generation Cambodian Americans. This volume is dedicated to all Cambodians and Cambodian Americans who persist in creatively writing from the margins.

NHLA is a non-governmental organization established in 2002 to support a new generation of Cambodians interested in literary expression: poetry and fiction. Both writers associated with the founding of the association, YIN Luoth and KHEM Akhaing, have served as advisers from its inception. Their dedication is deeply appreciated.

Since 2002 writers from Great Britain, Sweden, Australia, Malaysia and the United States have volunteered to give NHLA workshops on poetry, short fiction, screenplay and the art of editing to young writers in Cambodia. These magnanimous volunteers include K.S. Maniam, Geoffrey Charles Ryman, Bunkong Tuon, Laura Jean McKay, Anna Mattsson, Jeanne Morel, Alex Ratanapratum, and Horatio Potter among others. Professors Tomoko Okada (Japan) and Klairung Amratisha (Thailand) have also contributed their expertise to this project. In 2015 Fulbright Student Scholar and creative writer Colin Hodgkins lead a very successful six-month workshop for short-fiction writing in English while novelist and screenplay writer Larry Chambers lead a screenplay writing workshop, both in Phnom Penh. These volunteers have made a deep impression on a new generation of writers in Cambodia, where there are still no creative writing programs in universities.

Finally, I wish to express special thanks to poet YENG Chheangly for his ongoing support of NHLA, and to my translation partner and NHLA office manager NHIM Soknea, also to Natalie Desantiago for copy editing, and Ann Chau for superior management skills enabling me to complete this manuscript. This volume exists due to their assistance and goodwill.

Introduction:
Writing from the Margins
Teri Shaffer Yamada

Check any reference work on Southeast Asia for its entry on "Contemporary Cambodian Literature." Most likely, there is none. By 2016, however, there are creative writers and poets in Cambodia actively producing literary works, mostly from the margins of public culture. Why?

A Late Start

It is true that Cambodia got a delayed start in developing modern literature compared to those areas of Southeast Asia colonized or heavily influenced by the British, Dutch, or Spanish. Cambodia was part of the French Protectorate known as Indochine (1887), also including Laos and Vietnam.

The French were particularly enamored with the long, sophisticated literary tradition they discovered in Vietnam with its deep roots in Chinese culture. They considered Laos and Cambodia, with their scripts based on Sanskrit, as backwaters of tradition frozen in times past. So they were late in introducing the necessary technology and institutions for the emergence of modern literature: print culture in the form of printing presses, vernacular language newspapers, and a broad public school infrastructure. The first Cambodian novellas, the preferred genre of fiction, appeared in the late 1930s and 1940s, frequently serialized in newspapers or literary magazines. These novellas, like Rim Kin's *Suphat* (1938), were often socially critical tales of romantic love.

Various literary genres—including essays and short stories—along with a small literate public emerged in the 1940s and early 1950s especially in urban centers like Phnom Penh. Among the famous novelists of this period, the diplomat and writer Nou Hach (1917-75) published socially critical essays in several literary magazines. Among his novels, the tragic romance *Phka Srabon* (The Faded Flower, 1947) remained part of the public high school curriculum for decades. That era of cultural creativity, still romanticized as modern Cambodia's Golden Age, tragically ends in the 1970s.

A Tradition of Censorship

From the emergence of nationalism at the end of the nineteenth century, writer-journalists in Southeast Asia were strategic players in organizing political movements through newspapers, fiction, and other means of communication. Cambodia was no exception.

Nationalism in Cambodia developed unevenly. Both the French and their endorsed Cambodian monarchy imposed censorship laws on the press and writers. The appearance of black-clad Khmer Rouge cadres in Phnom Penh on April 17, 1975 signified a new regime of repression. The Khmer Rouge period of social control (1975-79) illustrates total state power over literary production. The literature they allowed was largely limited to ideologically formulaic revolutionary songs and forced confessions.

Although Khmer Rouge cadres would conspicuously display confiscated ballpoint pens in their shirt pockets as a symbol of power, they did not like writers, who were found mostly among the educated bourgeois "new people." Only a score of writers and intellectuals survived the experience of starvation, disease or torture under the Pol Pot regime. When the Vietnamese finally invaded Cambodia in 1979, many of the surviving writers fled to France where, over the next several decades, they would develop a distinct Cambodian literary tradition in exile. A few writers eventually relocated to the United States, such as Soth Polin and U Sam Oeur, but they would have difficulty publishing their works due to the small population interested in Khmer fiction or poetry in the United States. The remaining handful of well-known literary survivors became part of the new government established by the Vietnamese, the People's Republic of Kampuchea (PRK).

viii   *Modern Literature of Cambodia*

As Cambodian literature in diaspora basically developed in two forms—either poetry or testimonial discourse about the atrocities and emotional consequences of the Khmer Rouge era—literature in Cambodia remained politically constrained. Under the PRK all novels had to be vetted and approved by a state agency before being produced through state publishing houses. Politically correct, social realist novels occupied the entire field of Cambodia's official literary production during the PRK 1980s. One exception is Vandy Kaon's novella *Devils Island*, a cleverly disguised allegory of state corruption, which slipped past state censors.

Although many state-sponsored novels were published during the 1980s, their formulaic content did not appeal to readers eager for entertainment. Unauthorized rental shops appeared in private homes or black markets to meet this demand. Writers used pen names for protection, and their novels of different genres were reproduced as hand-written manuscripts.   These were widely circulated and reached the outlying provinces, even the Thai border camps. The popular female writer Pal Vannarirak is one of these underground novelists. Meanwhile, Cambodians in diaspora—from Australia to France—produced over forty autobiographies on the atrocities of the Khmer Rouge era and its legacy of sorrow. Bunkong Tuon's essay "On Fathers, Losses, and Other Influences" in this volume reflects such sentiment.

Cambodia finally gained independence after democratic elections supervised by the United Nations Transitional Authority in Cambodia (UNTAC, 1992-3). Mass media now became a part of Cambodia's information culture. A new generation of writers, born after 1975 and with little memory of the Khmer Rouge era, published short fiction in the scores of independent newspapers that proliferated in some larger cities, especially Phnom Penh. The short story "Just A Human Being" by Anonymous (Yamada 2013) exemplifies the type of socially critical fiction often published in newspapers of the '90s, and the need for the author to use a pen name for protection. In 1997 Hun Sen overthrew the democratically elected government of Cambodia. He continues to exert political control over the public right to dissent and the judicial system.

Writers and journalists still must be very cautious about freely expressing their views in newspapers or fiction. In 2000, writer Kong Bunchhoeun, known both for his song lyrics and fiction, received the prestigious S.E.A. Write Award for his novel *The Destiny of Tat Samarina*. The story was based on an actual acid attack involving the jealous wife of an important government official and her victim, Kong's niece. Kong also received death threats because of this novel and no longer lives in Cambodia.

New Possibilities and Ongoing Challenges

In 2016, Cambodian writers continue to confront the significant financial burden of self-publishing, poor distribution networks, widespread book piracy, and fear of political violence if they are too famous and too critical of the government. Writing from the cultural margins, outside the public spotlight, provides some sense of protection for emerging young writers who explore socially critical issues in their poetry and fiction.

One frequent theme in contemporary literature is the "immorality" of the extreme gap between the rich and the poor. Poet Yeng Chheangly's "Strobe Lights" (2013) in this collection contrasts the exclusive interior of a nightclub, with its glittery strobe lights and happy people, to the darkness of the outside world populated by the impoverished and uneducated. Chin Meas, a Buddhist monk for many years, reflects upon the greed unleashed upon the environment with mass deforestation changing the climate. In her short story "Suicide Plan" (2013), Seng Chanmonirath confronts the selfishness of the new class of privileged youth in Phnom Penh in contrast to the extremely poor beggars they ignore in their city. This theme is elliptically expressed in Sun Try's fantasy story "Exhibition Year 3333" (2013). Women's socio-economic status, especially the unintended consequences of arranged

x   *Modern Literature of Cambodia*

marriage, is a common theme for young writers along with political or bureaucratic corruption. In Heng Oudom's "I Repeat a Level" (2011), the protagonist refuses to bribe his high school teacher and thus fails to move up to the next grade level. The culture of bribes remains endemic in Cambodia.

Several writers' associations, including the Nou Hach Literary Association (2002), attempt to provide a safer space for writers to freely express their ideas. The 2013 S.E.A. Write Award recipient Sok Chanphal, whose stories like "Just a Dream with a Bad Ending," found in this collection, take place with a karmic twist on the gritty streets of Phnom Penh. With the help of his literary friends, Sok has recently opened a neighborhood library-cafe—Bonnalai Café— near a public school close to the Russian Market in Phnom Penh to foster a culture of reading. There are no neighborhood public libraries in Cambodia. Most libraries are associated with universities or local non-governmental organizations like SIPAR, which fosters reading by lending books through its traveling van libraries.

Cambodia now has the largest population of college educated citizens and readers in its history. It has young writers who express themselves well in poetry, novels and short fiction. Among this new generation of highly educated Cambodians are those trained in the private international schools of Phnom Penh. They are writing in English. Among these younger writers, many hope for literary fame and some do succeed. Suong Mak's novel *Boyfriend* (2010), a gay love story set in Phnom Penh, became popular from its beginning as a blog. However, blogging culture, while especially vibrant in Phnom Penh, faces censorship with the passage of new Internet restrictions.

What remains true is that Cambodian writers do exist. In Cambodia they write and publish from the margins, whether through small print runs or narrative techniques that conceal direct criticism of corruption in the institutions running the country. Many continue the admired oral story-telling tradition of Cambodia through performance art.

Recommended Reading

Nette, Andrew. 2014. "A New Wave of Cambodian Writers." *Australian Author* 46.2:10-13.

Yamada, Teri, ed. 2013. *'Just a Human Being' and Other Tales from Contemporary Cambodia.* Charleston, S.C.: Nou Hach Literary Association.

———, ed. 2002. "Modern Short Fiction in Cambodia: A History of Persistence," in *Modern Short Fiction of Southeast Asia: A Literary History,* ed. Teri Yamada, pp. 111-152.

CONTENTS

Introduction: Writing from the Margins / vi
 Teri Shaffer Yamada

Short Fiction from Cambodia

1. Just a Dream with a Bad Ending / 1
    Sok Chanphal
2. Bad Karma / 10
    Sok Chanphal
3. A Suicide Plan / 16
    Seng Chanmonirath
4. A Daughter's Tears / 21
    Kao Sokchea
5. Girl in a Pink Dress (1), (2) / 26
    Than Chan Tepi
6. Season's End for a Lady of the Night / 33
    Noch Sakona
7. I Repeat a Level / 42
    Heng Oudom
8. Exhibition Year 3333 / 47
    Sun Try
9. Becoming Young Again / 49
    Sun Try
10. Starlight / 51
    Chieb Kim Heang
11. Ghost Environment / 58
    Ry Sarong

Poetry and Essays from Cambodia

12. Poetry by Chin Meas
    Piggybank / 62
    Rahula Swallows the Moon / 63
    Remote Control / 63

13. Poetry by Yeng Chheangly
     Strobe Lights / 64
     Recycle Bottle Collector / 65
14. Poetry by Suy Vansak
     A Warrior's Spirit / 66
15. Poetry by Venerable Kreun Yoeun
     Buffaloes / 67
16. Essay by Sophiline Cheam Shapiro
     Dancing Stories / 69

Poetry and Essays by Cambodian Americans

17. Essay and Poetry by Yin Luoth
     As a Poet: An Essay / 75
     Poor Boy in a Modern Time / 77
     Modern Rice Field / 78
     Mekong River / 78
     Lexus / 79
     My Neighbors / 79
18. Essay and Poetry by Bunkong Tuon
     On Fathers, Losses, and Other Influences: Essay / 80
     Inheritance / 92
     The Day My Worst Fear Came True / 93
19. Poetry by PraCh
     art of faCt / 96
     The Great EsCape! / 100
20. Poetry by Kelley Peng
     Hystory of a DREAM / 103

A Play by Cambodian Americans

21. The Unraveling Truth: A Play in Four Acts / 107

SHORT FICTION FROM CAMBODIA

1

SOK Chanphal is a contemporary fiction and songwriter located in Phnom Penh. Born in 1984 in Kampong Cham province, he graduated in 2010 with a B.A. in International Communications from the Human Resource University in Phnom Penh. SOK started his writing career in 2007 as an editor and has worked as a lyricist for Hang Meas Production since 2009. He has won a number of literary awards including the prestigious S.E.A. Write Award for Cambodia in 2013. SOK Chanphal has published a number of short story and song lyric collections, and novellas. The theme of karmic consequences runs through many of his short stories.

Just a Dream with a Bad Ending
Sok Chanphal

Today is Saturday—an annoying, bad day.... I still remember what my manager said to me. That idiot scolded me saying: "Why didn't you show up for work yesterday?"

"Yes! I wasn't well, and I'd called to ask permission!" I responded politely, which is different from what I was thinking. I wanted to yell: *What are you asking me again for when I'd already gotten permission?*

"How are you able to work today?"

I stared at him briefly then responded politely. "Today, I'm feeling better!"

"What did you have that you recovered so quickly?"

What! Is it a problem that I got well so soon? But I replied politely: "Headache, sir."

"If it was just a headache, you should have been able to

2 Modern Literature of Cambodia

come to work anyway; aren't you man enough?"

I just bowed my head respectfully and remained silent while waiting for my crazy boss to continue speaking: "We had piles of work, but you didn't come in! I'm not stupid, I know...".

Just as he finished, his phone rang. His face changed to a happy expression as he answered the phone: "Hello, my darling!...". But his expression switched to disappointment since she'd already hung up. Then he called her back and spoke sweetly to her, a young woman the same age as his youngest daughter. He talked for six or seven minutes, then said: "Let's stop now! I have a meeting... I'll see you after work!"

Such a playboy! It was boring for me to overhear his flirting with a girl. This girl was just flirting with him because of his money! I'm a handsome young man, but they don't even look at me.

"What were we just talking about?" My boss asked me... Oh, I've been demeaning my boss without telling you his name: Noriey.

"After you leave work, you will go pick her up," I responded literally to his question.

"I want to talk about you!" He yelled at me.

"Yes! You finished saying that you were not stupid...".

"That's right!" He cut me off: "In short, we can see no future for you based on how you work everyday. If you are so good at being sick, be careful, you may be out of a job. Now go back to your desk and get to work. The big boss has us under a lot of pressure. Next week there will be a meeting with an overseas company. You must get everything done!"

The phone is ringing again and he wants me to leave the room. His command made me feel so angry that I wanted to choke him to death. He looked down at me as I was silent. I'm sick but cannot ask permission to leave! If he gets sick, he will ask permission for a week off to spend with his girlfriend. I guarantee it. I don't think anyone can choose when they will get sick? When he says things like this, I just want to cut out his tongue. I can't stand it any longer! It doesn't matter if I have a job, I'm not staying under his control any longer. He's threatening to fire me! Who else can do this job? Idiot boss! Every day, always talking on his phone, flirting with young women. And he gives me all the work. Seems like he uses me just like an animal. I'm furious. Because I need money and I don't know of any other place to work, I'm forced to stay here under this physical and mental pressure.

Hopeless! I can't stay like this; I have to change it. I'm not a tree or an animal that just allows anyone to abuse it. This job is like hell! I must quit! What makes me the angriest is how he tells me I have no future. What future anyway? In the future we all die! He acts like a fortuneteller; is that why he predicts other people's futures? I can't tolerate this. *The one who has no future is you!*

I left the office and let the ghosts do the work instead of me. I went home to sleep still angry with my boss Noriey. What's happened to my life? Why am I so miserable? What should I do? I don't blame myself, but I blame my cruel boss. In this company, I was next in the line of command beneath him. He doesn't know anything. He always does something bad to me at work and benefits from my effort. His kind of knowledge is self-serving. If I became the boss, maybe this company would improve tenfold. But my boss is stupid like a cow. He doesn't know which employee is competent or not. He is using company money for bribes! What a mess! The people in this company don't perceive that I am capable. They let Noriey hurt me. Now I'm not letting him hurt me any longer since the one out of a job is me! The bad person is Noriey. Even if he doesn't have a future, I will. If I can't make a decision, I shouldn't be a boss! Kill him! I must kill Noriey!

But how am I going to kill him? Easy! He's a passionate playboy! I'll just find a beautiful girl with AIDS to flirt with him, then infect him. Hah, hah, hah! Noriey will get sick and die. And the murderer is AIDS; no one will know who is behind this. Hah, hah, hah!

No. I can't do that! Someone with AIDS may take a long time to die, and my boss has a lot of money so he can

4   *Modern Literature of Cambodia*

buy medicine to stop it, or get blood transfusions, or work out to improve his health. He surely can live longer. And I'll end up living a painful life because I'll still be under his control. Gosh! He needs to die soon so that I can take over his position and have a good future. What should I do? If I hire a killer, it might not be a safe plan. I wonder if a better plan would be to put poison in his coffee? No! That's too awful! The innocent, honest person who poured the coffee would be blamed.

...the plan is done! I can't let anyone know about it. I'm afraid they will tell others!

.   .   .   .

My plan to kill him has begun...Sunday morning, Noriey is staying alone at his villa outside the city waiting for his girlfriend Chorvey. I telephone her: "Hello, Chorvey. My boss is asking you to wait for him at a five-star hotel for a change of scene. You don't need to go to his villa outside the city."

"My... he thinks of strange things," Chorvey said laughing. "Okay, bye."

"Okay, that's it!"

"Thank you so much, my dear Snaay. One day I will call you for a date! Bye!"

I smile cruelly then start trembling, afraid that Chorvey will call Noriey so my plan will be ruined. I begin to implement my plan immediately. The sunlight spills over my head, like the lamp on the headboard of my bed. I call a motorcycle taxi and he drives me to Noriey's villa. I have him stop at a distance from the villa and I walk over to it alone. I don't want the driver to see me enter that house. I press the doorbell. It rings and then the door opens. Noriey is at the door, surprised, "Is it you?"

I pretend, saying: "Yes, boss! I have an important matter to discuss with you!"

"What would that be? It's Sunday." *He acts so rudely*

to me just like before. No matter! Shortly you'll act like this again,

I reply politely: "This matter is related to your embezzling money from the company…".

He looks shocked and stays silent, letting me continue with my trickery. The big boss tells me: "I already know about this." Then he asks me to clarify.

Noriey's eyes have become as white as a boiled fish's. Then I said: "Let's go into the house and I will tell you the whole story."

He walks trembling before me into his home. I laugh while I glare at his back. Just as we enter, the telephone rings. I rush to stop him from answering the phone, saying: "Don't pick it up."

He cancels the call, and looks at me. I laugh evilly.

"A knife!" he yells.

"That's right, it's a knife," I smile, laughing.

"What are you going to do, Snaay?"

As he asks, he presses his phone on as the knife leaves my hand. The blood gushes out of a vein in his hand as he drops the phone. He is so frightened, like a fly falling down into shampoo.

I laugh: "Haa, haa! Are you scared? Why don't you blame this jerk again?" I wanted to say "me" but referred to myself in pejorative slang.

"What are you going to do," my boss speaks with trembling lips.

"I want to kill…! Haa, haa … kill people… haaa, haaa… specifically you."

"Why….why…you… to…to…k..ill me?" He stutters.

"Haa! Haa! Why are you trembling? I want to kill you because you always hurt me. Haa, haa, haa. Why don't you yell at me again?"

"I've stopped, Snaay!" He says, lowering to his knees on the floor to beg me.

I reply, "I'm not Mr. Bao Jintien in a Chinese movie. But if you are getting down on your knees like this, I'd like you to

6   *Modern Literature of Cambodia*

elucidate your mistakes as I listen. Please confess to all the bad things you've done to me."

Noriey begins to confess and beg: "I looked down on you! I always did bad things to you! I asked you to do a lot of extra work, which benefited me. I…I…was really awful. I could confess all evening without finishing."

"So where is your refrigerator? I want some orange juice and cake to eat while I listen to your confession."

"Yes, the kitchen is over there. Go straight and turn left; you'll see it."

"Hah, Hah. You think I'm stupid? Keep talking, then I will kill you."

"…I…I…recognize my mistakes. Please forgive me, nephew."

"Nephew! I'm not your nephew! I'm someone you look down on."

"Nephew, please take pity on me. I'm old. I can't live much longer. Everyday I did bad things due to the short time left in my life."

"Like you are a philosopher now? You want me to feel excited about your speech? No way."

"Nephew, please take pity on me. I want to see my youngest daughter married before I die. Then, I can die. But now I cannot."

"Your youngest daughter will become someone's mistress, like your young play girls. You don't need to wait for your daughter's painful future."

"No! Even though I play around with a lot of young girls, I love my daughter. Snaay, if you don't kill me, I will change, make myself into a better man. I'll stop hurting you. I know a lot about life now!"

"Oh, if you understand it so well, die now! You don't need to stay alive."

"From now on my life is for the nation and my family. I will stop doing bad things. Nephew, you should understand fatherly feelings. I want to see my daughter happy."

"Don't mess around with me. You've been talking

about your daughter and family, but where are the tears? You are just talking about them to stay alive."

"Oh, I know! If you don't kill me, I'll marry my daughter to you."

"Oh yeah! Your daughter is beautiful like Miss Universe. If I had a wife as beautiful as that, maybe… "

"Die, you creep!" he yelled and stabbed at me with a knife. He thinks I've lost focus because of his daughter's beauty. I grab his hand and push him back.

"Hum! I don't want to be your son-in-law," I say.

"Snaay, don't kill me. I beg you. I will give you my entire fortune."

I stood up properly and stared at my boss who seemed incapable of doing anything. Then I felt so surprised. Yikes! I've been playing around with him up until now. Maybe someone will come and wreck my plans to kill him. I rudely speak: "Say your last words! No more talking. You're wasting time!"

"Snaay!!"

The knife makes a distinctive sound as it repeatedly pierces his chest. My knife penetrates his heart three times. There is no way that he can be alive. I told him to say his last words but he called out my name instead…. Hey! If I'd known, I would have told him to say ten words. Maybe he would have told me where he kept his valuables. This is regrettable….but, whatever; perhaps that would have just made his ghost haunt me.

I don't remove the knife from his body. Barely breathing, he then dies with his eyes open. I laugh: "Haa, haa, haa!"

.   .   .   .

Everything I've told you is just a dream.

When I wake up, I'm terrified and covered in sweat. My

8   Modern Literature of Cambodia

plan to kill my boss came true but only in a dream. Noriey, the person I hate the most, died in my dream... when I think back to all the things that happened in my dream, I become frightened of myself: *Awful!! I am so cruel.*

So tomorrow I will be sitting at my desk, looking at folders, and thinking *I want to resign.* No one will call or maybe no one needs me. I don't care about my salary or about what anyone else thinks. This must end! But how can I find another job? I've been thinking that I want to get married next year. But how can I if I quit my job? And If I want to marry a wealthy woman, she will not consider me without a job. But if I marry a poor woman, we may become beggars together. I'm so depressed.

"Hello," I answer the phone.

"...Snaay...Snaay. Come to my house!"

Whose voice? Noriey's. I rush to put down the phone. Why did he call me about coming to his house? I will not go just to let him blame me for something. I'm okay about losing my job ... maybe he's called me to beg me not to quit? Maybe he wants to give me a raise? Then he will confess all his mistakes to me just like in my dream.

I'm eating noodles while I think. Without finishing them, I decide to drive my motorcycle to his villa outside of town. The gate is ajar like he might have left it open for me. The door to the house is also open. Maybe he is waiting for me inside? I walk into the house and see him slumped on the floor.

"Boss! Is it a heart attack, high blood pressure?"

I turn him face up. Then I see that a knife has been stabbed into his chest. Noriey is already dead. No! I must just be dreaming? How could he be dead? When he called me his voice was trembling. That means someone must have been threatening him. Who killed him?

When I turn around, four or five policemen are walking toward me. When I look at my hands, I see they are covered in blood. I can barely speak: "No, no... I didn't kill him!"

The police say to me: "Confess now and we will take you to the police station.

I raise my hands up and keep saying: "I didn't kill him."

One of the policemen puts handcuffs on my wrists and escorts me to jail. They accuse me of murder, intent to kill Noriey out of revenge for his blaming me yesterday. I only reply: "It's just a dream with a bad ending."

.   .   .   .

I was in jail for two years until they found the real murderer who killed Noriey. It was one of the staff he'd bullied and fired. Losing his job, the guy became enraged and killed him. But in my case, it was merely a plan and a dream that got me jailed for two years.

Translated by Teri Yamada and NHIM Soknea

2

Bad Karma
Sok Chanphal

I'm driving my motorbike when I stop at a traffic light and notice two traffic control officers. Yesterday both of them had stopped me and demanded money, accusing me of running a red light.

"Take out your driver's license!" one of the policeman demanded as he removed the starter key from my motorbike.

"What did I do?" I asked wondering.

"Didn't you see the red light a moment ago?"

"No! It was still green. That's why I kept going."

"Don't talk so much. Just take out your driver's license."

"Why do I need to take out my license?"

"What's the problem? Don't you have one?"

"My license is at home. I forgot to bring it with me."

"So go get it!"

"Why do I need to go home to get it? I didn't do anything wrong? A moment ago, I crossed the light with other traffic. Why are you stopping only me?"

"Just do as I say! Go talk to the other policeman!" He pointed to a policeman standing near a motorbike, with a pen and ticket book in his hands.

"Now if you want to make it easy, you pay; if not, you go study traffic law?" The policeman posed this question to me.

I replied, "Of course, I want to make it easy."

"So, pay me 20,000 riel."

"Twenty thousand riel? That's making it easy? A moment ago I crossed the street on a green light but when you stopped me, the light became red. Do you understand?"

"What, you want to study? I'll register you for traffic

"Bad Karma"   11

school then!"

"I don't think so, please talk rationally. I'm in a hurry for a job interview!"

"Interview or not, I don't care; pay me 20,000 riel."

"Why do I need to pay you when I'm not in the wrong?"

"If you don't want to pay, what's your name?" The policeman talked with a frown. He spoke to the other policeman: "Phan, take his name down."

I became so angry my hand started to tremble. I wanted to punch him in the face. The policeman called Phan whispered to me: "Just give him whatever money you have."

"Give what? To make it easy? The police should be reasonable, otherwise it's called robbery."

"What, how rude! Now you'll go to the police station where you'll get stronger advice!" Said the policeman who had originally demanded the 20,000 riel.

I stood there and remained silent while watching them demand money from other motorists. Some motorists were giving 20,000 riel, some 10,000 riel, and others 5,000 riel. I was so angry but also anxious as I looked at my cell phone and noticed it was time for my interview. I couldn't protest this so I decide to go the easy way with them like the other motorists.

I spoke to both of them: "I have only 5,000 riel." I handed the money over saying: "Give me the key to my motorbike."

Phan was ready to return my motorbike key, but the other policeman yelled at him, "I'm not letting him go for 5,000 riel. For rude people, even 20,000 riel isn't enough."

I clenched my teeth and felt sorry that I'd told them I was in a hurry to get to an interview. It allowed them to act even worse to me. I didn't want this bad experience to interfere with my chance of getting a job. I gave them another 5,000 riel. But the policeman acted like he didn't care and spoke with a frown: "For a person like you, if I make it too easy this time, you'll just do it again."

Even though I'm angry, I need to force myself to give

12   *Modern Literature of Cambodia*

them 10,000 more riel because I need to hurry to my interview. I drive off on my motorbike feeling revengeful and intensely angry.

When I arrive at the company for my interview, my name is crossed off the list. I beg them to give me a chance, explaining why I was late; but they wouldn't accept my excuse. The job that I'd dreamed about for so long is now lost, and I can't get it back even though I'd passed the writing test and only the interview remained.

I feel sorry that I lost this job, and I'm so angry with the two policemen that I can't sleep all night. All my mishaps are due to these bad policemen. If I don't take revenge, it is unjust to me. If I can take revenge on them, surely there will be someone to thank me. Those who do unjust deeds will meet bad karmic consequences. But if we wait for a deity to punish them, we don't know when it will happen. I will be the divine messenger sent by a deity to punish these evildoers.

So that is the reason why today I've stopped my motorcycle by the traffic light. I see the same two police officers stopping motorists and demanding money. No matter. I plan to make them demand money from me again. I'm staring at the green light with the numbers running down, waiting until the red light begins so I can drive across.

I'm waiting for the red light. I intend to ride my motorbike slowly to make them stop me. Just as I thought, the policemen are gesturing at me to stop. My hands are trembling, but this is a good chance for me. I pretend I'm going to stop but then rev up the motorbike and take off...

.   .   .   .

There is bad karma in this world, which happens in this life not the next. There is cause and effect. All of the story I've relayed so far is just the beginning; the plot is not yet concluded. One year later, a story that started out like a joke has become a tragedy.

One day, while I was driving my motorcycle to work, I

"Bad Karma" 13

hit a newspaper boy knocking him down. All the newspapers scattered around him while he couldn't move, then he attempted to stand up. I parked my motorbike, collected all the newspapers, and then carried him to the sidewalk. I'm so unlucky; but if I just left him lying there, I'd be such a bad person.

I grasped the boy's hand and saw how badly he was bleeding. I said to him: "Please forgive me! I'll take you to the hospital."

This boy was about ten years old. I looked at his face and wanted to cry. But he didn't blame me, saying: "Don't worry! I must continue selling my newspapers!"

I told him, "Don't worry. I'll buy them all. Please let me take you to the hospital!"

The little boy hesitated and said, "If you are going to a hospital, please take me to my father."

I followed his directions. Along the way, I asked: "Is your father a doctor?"

"No, my father's a patient there," the little boy replied.

"Oh so that's it. What's wrong with your father?"

"He has mental problems. He forgets us and cannot remember; and when his illness worsens, he screams and cries...".

This child is just a little boy. And he is selling newspapers because of his father's mental illness. I ask him: "Do you go to school every day to study?"

"No. I sell newspapers and magazines all day long!"

"So this is the only way your family makes money?"

"My mother bakes cakes and my sister sells them. My sister and I never go to school because we need to earn money for my father's medical care."

This makes me cry. His family is very poor so he has no chance to study. The father, who is the head of the family, gets sick; is this karma or not? I think about what I could do to help this family. I ask this little boy: "Do you want to study?"

"I really want to but what can I do? I need to sell newspapers..."

14   *Modern Literature of Cambodia*

"You can ask your mother if you could sell only half day and take time to study at school the other half."

"You don't know? My mother owes a lot of money because of my father's medical bills. And now my mother tries to   earn more money to repay them and also pay the monthly hospital bill. If I go to school, I cannot learn anything because I'm so worried."

I took a long breath after listening to him and asked: "What about your sister; how old is she?"

"I have two sisters. One is eight-years-old, the other is six."

"Does your six-year-old sister sell the cakes?"

"Yes!"

When I heard this story, I was speechless.   Maybe I need to find some organization somewhere to help this boy's family; what should I do? I felt sad about the boy's future without any education.   When he grows up, how will he survive?

"I studied up to the third grade. If my father hadn't gotten sick, my family would have been okay. And my sisters could also study." The boy says while looking upset.

"How did your father become sick?"

"A motorcycle hit him…".

I wondered who hit him making such bad fortune for this family.   Has that person been living happily while this family has been living in misery?

"Do you know who hit your father?" I asked the boy.

"No one knows. He left after hitting him. If that person had been as kind as you bringing me to the hospital, my mother would not have needed to borrow so much money."

"What caused the accident?"

"My father was working."

"What was his job?"

"He worked for the police."

"What kind of job?"

"Traffic officer!"

Having said this, the little boy pointed out the entrance

"Bad Karma" 15

to the hospital where his father was staying. Then he took me to his father.

"There is my father."

.   .   .   .

This is the kind of karma that I've been describing. The father of the pitiful boy is the police officer named Phan. My motorbike hit him last year. I can remember his face clearly, but he has lost his memory and cannot remember who did this bad thing to him and his family. When the boy ran to hold his father's hand and introduced me to him, I cried and was deeply embarrassed beyond description.

Still no one knows that I am the one who hit Mr. Phan. Now I'd like to remove all my bad karma. I give my entire salary to his family and support his children's education. I lie to them that an NGO is supporting them. And I have no idea how long it will take me to erase this bad karma.

Translated by Teri Yamada and NHIM Soknea

3

SENG Chanmonirath was born on November 20, 1995, in Kampot province and has been writing novels since the age of twelve. She was a senior in high school when she won the first place prize for short fiction in the 2013 Nou Hach Literary Awards competition. After graduating college, she intends to be a part-time writer.

A Suicide Plan
Seng Chanmonirath

I am very angry. My parents are so busy with their work that they neither care nor have time for me. So if they are making all this money, whom are they spending it on? They don't consider my feelings. Because I'm the daughter of wealthy parents, I'm always wasting time hanging out with friends. Now I've failed the college entrance exam unlike them. My boyfriend has also left me. He only wanted to use me. It makes me even more upset because my parents are arguing every time I go home. I try to help my parents solve their problems, but they blame me instead. I've already decided that I will find a place to kill myself because I want my parents to feel regret.

I don't know how my destiny will play out but it surprises me; the more I think about this, my life is just a joke. I try to find somewhere in my room to hang myself, but there is no good place for that so I go out. I discover some empty land just outside of Phnom Penh and park my motorbike to check it out. There is a tree that's suitable for hanging. I decide to hang myself on that tree but realize that I've forgotten to bring the rope. So I drive my motorbike around for

"A Suicide Plan" 17

a long time until I find a shop where I can buy some. I reach for the money in my pocket, but there isn't any. So I have to go back home first. Then I return with the rope to the lot where I plan to hang myself. I throw the rope over a branch of the big tree. I didn't know whether this is good or bad luck for me. I step up on a big rock and jump off to hang myself but the branch breaks and I fall down. I'm very angry and drive my motorbike back to the city.

I decide that this time, I'm really going to die. I drive my motorbike to a pharmacy to buy some poison, but they don't stock anything like that. So I go to another one, but they have run out. After I'm finally able to purchase some, I go to buy a big hamburger so I can put the poison inside it. I pour the liquid poison inside the hamburger and then start to eat it but throw up everything I've eaten so far that day when I see the liquid dripping out.

Now I've decided to jump off a tall building. I'm going to close my eyes and leap. But just as I'm about to jump, I hear someone talking near me on a phone, crying and saying: "We broke up, goodbye!" Just as he finishes saying this, he jumps. I'm stunned and open my eyes. There he is lying on the ground below surrounded by a crowd. I feel really scared and angry. That guy killed himself before me even though I wanted to die. I couldn't go look at him because there were so many people surrounding him.

I decide to drive my motorbike to Chhroy Changvar Bridge to jump off. When I get there, I look in both directions and then step up on the railing, but my stomach growls because I'm so hungry having vomited up everything before. I decide that if I'm going to die, I should at least be full first. I decide to drive to the Riverside to find something to eat.

I find a parking place and stop there to count my money. I start walking across but stumble and fall. I stand up really angry, look around and see an old beggar. Unable to walk since he has no legs, he moves with his one good hand by using a board with wheels.

When I see him, I rush to apologize since I'd almost

18   *Modern Literature of Cambodia*

fallen on him.

"Grandfather! I'm so sorry. I apologize. I didn't see you!"

"Don't worry about it."

His voice is barely audible. Then he uses his hand to slowly move the wheeled board away with much difficulty. He looks at me so pitifully. Then I take out my money and give him four 5,000 riel notes, placing them in his hat because I know that I'll be dying soon.

When he notices me giving him so much money, he says: "Granddaughter, thanks for giving me so much money! Many thanks." And then he says: "You are a good person. I wish you good luck."

I leave smiling because I don't need good luck any more.   But just then it occurs to me that I want to ask him two or three questions so I return.   I squat down to ask him: "Grandfather, don't be angry with me. I want to ask you some questions."

"No problem."

"Can you tell me why you ask people for money?"

"It's not that I want to beg for money; it's due to my physical condition. I have no choice. I never went to school. I need money for food. Life is a struggle! Granddaughter, I also want to stay alive to see how the world develops so I must depend on people who pity me enough to give me money. I cannot survive by myself. You are a good person. You still have a chance and the ability to succeed so you must struggle to overcome difficulties in your life."

"Don't you feel upset about your condition?"

"Yes, but what can I do about it? If I get upset, does it bring back my feet or arm?   I just try to understand this and encourage myself to live."

"You have so many more difficulties than I do, but I'm so much more upset than you are."

"What is your difficulty? You have so much because you are healthy. Why do you say you have such difficulty? What about me? Don't be so hopeless?"

"A Suicide Plan"   19

"Grandfather. I appreciate what you've said."

"Don't appreciate a beggar. Try to make your life more beautiful than mine. Goodbye?"

He finishes his speech and rolls away. I feel ashamed about what he has said. I'm not looking at him anymore like a beggar. I observe him even longer until I start feeling hungry.

I find a porridge seller and eat two bowls of porridge since I'm so hungry from vomiting up everything I'd eaten earlier. While eating the porridge, I notice a girl staring at me. I want to escape her attention, but she keeps staring at me. I call to her: "Come here, sister!"

She won't come closer. I try calling her many times, and she finally approaches me. The little girl looks really hungry. Her clothes are dirty rags. I start to ask: "Aren't you hungry?"

She nods "yes" instead of replying. I tell the porridge seller to give her a bowl. The little girl starts to devour it. It looks like she's hungrier than me. I ask her: "Sister, what grade are you in?"

"I don't go to school."

"Where are your parents?"

"They're dead."

"So whom are you living with?"

"My grandma." The little girl finishes part of the porridge and puts the rest in a plastic bag. I try to stop her from leaving.

"Why don't you finish all of it?"

"I'm taking it to my grandmother and two younger siblings."

When I hear this, I'm shocked. This little girl cares about others more than herself, but I don't care. What about me? Do I care about other people around me? Now my parents are probably worrying about me. Am I considering their feelings? They told me not to have a boyfriend since I had to study so hard. But did I listen to them? No. They are fighting with each other because of me. Why haven't I thought about this problem? But instead I get a little angry and want to

20   *Modern Literature of Cambodia*

kill myself. I failed the exam because I didn't study. I don't need to blame anyone else. I'm thinking about the beggar's words again. He has neither health nor wealth, but he still wants to live and struggles to maintain his life. What about me? I have a beautiful healthy body and a much better life so why do I want to die? No, life is valuable and cannot be bought. I don't want to die. I miss my parents. I cannot leave them.

I ask the seller to pack up three portions of porridge, eight fertilized eggs and twenty grilled beef sticks for the little girl. I also give her some money; then I walk away in tears missing my parents. Everyone is staring at me.

I want to take off on my motorbike, but I suddenly see my fearful parents walking toward me. I just start crying not giving them a chance to ask me any questions.

"Mom and dad, I've made you worry so much!"

My father hugs me and says: "Foolish daughter. Do you know we've been looking everywhere for you?"

"I'm sorry. I will be a better daughter and not make you worry anymore. I will try to study again and not make you argue because of me."

"Alright. It makes me very happy that you will do this. Stop crying now."

My parents have no idea what I've been doing, but they are very happy to see me. They don't ask any questions just look at each other and smile. We all go home with such joy.

Since then I've searched for the beggar but could never find him. I always tell other people: "I felt I had a terrible life until I met all those pitiable people."

First published in the *Nou Hach Literary Journal*, Vol. 7, 2013.
Translated by Teri Yamada and NHIM Soknea

4

KAO Sokchea was born on April 17, 1991. She is a graduate of the Royal University of Phnom Penh majoring in Khmer Literature and hopes to continue writing informally while pursuing a career in radio journalism. Her next project is a novella. Her short story, "A Daughter's Tears," represents a new form of socially critical feminist writing in twenty-first century Cambodian literature and the theme of "development."

A Daughter's Tears
Kao Sokchea

In a typical dry season, it hardly ever rains— but sometimes it does. This is normal. The situation we want to happen doesn't and the one we don't want to does. Actually everyone tries to do their best, in hopes that something good will happen in return. But we never know when this good result is going to occur.

I just woke up and feel very rested today, perhaps because I'm in my parent's home. Also, I just graduated with a major in finance and banking from a university in Phnom Penh. My dream is to be the best banker in Cambodia. After I relax at home for one or two months, I'll continue studying and working. Gosh, there is nothing happier than my dreams coming true.

When I arrived home I was very stressed and depressed, but now that's disappeared. Whenever I'm back home, I never want to return to Phnom Penh, but my own desires ultimately make me want to leave here. My motivation is for my family, society, and me. After I become successful, I'll return to help develop my community. I've accomplished so much because of the encouragement and support of my par-

22   *Modern Literature of Cambodia*

ents and siblings. I think I am lucky to be born in this family with its genuine happiness. Who knows how many people are as lucky as me?

I eat *Samlakakaur* (palm fruit and vegetable stew) and grilled fish with fish sauce and lime until my stomach feels like bursting. This   local food symbolizes my family and community.   After having dinner,   my whole family talks together, chatting happily outside about a variety of things under the moonlight of the fifteenth day of the lunar month. As we talk, my father asks me a number of questions.

"Nee! Actually we've been wanting to tell you for a while; but since you just graduated, we wanted you to relax. So that's why we didn't tell you."

"What's the matter! Why so secretive?"

My father responds: "A few months ago the Sombhett family proposed an engagement between you and their son. I observed that the son has a good character and is obedient. And his family has a good reputation.   Your mother and I also discussed this and agreed that you would marry him after graduation."

I'm stunned to hear this. Why is father doing this to me? He didn't ask me if I agree. And I reply: "What, dad! Why don't you ask me if I love him? And if I want to get married or not?"

My mother, who has remained silent, now says: "My daughter, you are already old; it's not appropriate for a daughter to be alone too long. And you are a girl so it's not appropriate to study too much. With what you've done so far, it is enough to get married. After you get married you will depend on your husband."

I am so disappointed about what my mother said. I reply to her: "Mother, this generation is not the same as yours in which a girl doesn't need to study and waits for a husband to feed her! In this generation a girl can do whatever a boy does. I don't want to get married; I want to study. I want to pursue my dreams."

When my mother hears this, she gets angry because

no one dares oppose her, not even my father; but she is also a loving mother. Previously I always did what she said, that's why she thought I would do whatever she decided. And I always do what she says, because my mother thinks she is always right.

Then my mother says: "No! I already confirmed with them. And your engagement ceremony is the day after tomorrow."

I feel so much pain, like I would vomit blood. I began to lower my voice in order to soothe them: "Mother, father— truly I don't want to get married. I want to study. Please, both of you, talk to them about cancelling this. I beg both of you to do just this for me. Please! Before, I did whatever you told me, but now I want to decide for myself. Will you allow this? Please!" I said kneeling in respect to them with my hands together in supplication.

"Daughter. We can't replace the slats in a bed once they've been broken; and we cannot find words to replace our commitment. Do you want your family to lose its reputation?"

I really want to tell them it isn't me who will make the family lose its reputation; it is they. I didn't dare say this because I was afraid they would get angry. I started to speak, but my father cut me off. "We want you to live with us, not by yourself in Phnom Penh. We love you; that's why we did this."

"I don't know how much you love me, but you are forcing me to marry a guy I don't love. Is that what you call loving me?"

After talking at cross-purposes, my mother says: "If you don't marry, I will die. I'll die from embarrassment of having a daughter like you. Is there any family with such a daughter? If you don't believe that I will die, go ahead and see."

Having said this, my mother returned to the house with my father. "A good daughter does not disobey her parents." I don't know of any family whose mother wants to arrange a marriage for her daughter so I can't estimate such goodness. And my mother dares to die if her daughter disobeys. She

24   Modern Literature of Cambodia

also blames me for not being a good daughter since I won't obey her.   My mother is the one who told me to study and I did that.   My mother wants me to dress a certain way and I do that.   And she begs me not to have a boy friend or hang out with boys and I always obey her.   Why is she saying now that I'm a disrespectful daughter?   So what kind of daughter do they call respectful and obedient?

I sit alone, thinking all night about what I should do? My future will be destroyed, and everything I used to consider my dreams will dissolve like salt in water.   Oh my gosh!   What is my karma that causes me to meet this situation?   I tearfully decide to go ahead with the engagement for the sake of my parents.   Why can't I make my own decisions about my own life; it doesn't belong to me.   This life belongs to my parents not me?   Why do they still think about traditional marriage?   I don't know how to find the answer to this question.

.   .   .   .

It's engagement day.   I just found out that the guy's family is richer than my own.   That's why my mother insisted on this.   When I look at him, he appears to be everything that my parents promised.   I hope he will always be a good husband.

After we are engaged for one month, both families hold the wedding party.   My mother is so happy, different from me. I am thinking about my future, what my life will be like after I get married.

.   .   .   .

Time has passed. It's one year since my marriage and I've already had a baby. I named my son Choulneitt. It's later in the year, and I've never experienced a happy marriage. My husband always goes out drinking and comes home late. Moreover, he also has several other wives. Sometimes he hits me. Although my life is like this, I never tell my parents.

I'm still hiding it.

One day my husband comes home drunk and starts blaming me for everything wrong in our marriage. This time I could not stay calm because I've tried to be a good wife, which he never acknowledges. So I answer back. And we shout at each other. The baby starts crying, and even the nanny cannot calm him. The argument escalates. My husband picks up a vase and throws it at me; but I don't know what happens next—I've lost consciousness. When I wake up, I'm in the hospital. I think the nanny must have brought me here.

As I open my eyes, the first people I see are my parents. They are crying. My mother says, "I was wrong. I misjudged him. I'm so sorry."

My tears fall as I reply: "Mother and father you aren't wrong!"

Since I am crying, I can't say any more to let them know how deeply hurt I am. This is a life experience I will never forget. I swear to myself that I will not use this old tradition to take over my children's lives.

After I get better, my mother tells me that the justice system has already punished my husband. From now on, I can choose my own life, one that really belongs to me.

Translated by Teri Yamada and NHIM Soknea, July 3, 2012

5

THAN Chan Tepi was born in 1997 in Phnom Penh. She enjoys writing fables that reflect society. Her hope for the future is to become an author of literature and scholar of economics. She is now a business student at Raffles International College in Cambodia. THAN represents the first generation of writers in Cambodia to write fiction in English.

Girl in a Pink Dress (1)
Than Chan Tepi

The boisterous music of a party a few buildings away pushes its way through the flaring holes and plaster cracks in the dilapidated walls of Chett's home, making the children's adrenalin rush with thrill and excitement. Every beat of the *boom tsh boom boom tsh* that blares through the party's loudspeakers sends Kheang and Pheak jumping from side to side, flapping their frail arms that makes their tiny hands wiggle like wings trying to escape the hold of hunger and exhaustion.

Chett scoffs at her siblings as they continue to jump around to the beat of the music.

She returns to sweeping the crooked, creaking plank floor where they just had their usual dinner of cold leftover rice and rotten *prahok*—the floor that will soon become their bed for the night. Kheang and Pheak throw their pillows, race to Chett, and begin tugging on her loose worn-out pants and arms as she collects the pile of dirt and sweeps it into the dustpan. Chett scowls as she pushes them away.

"What is it? Can't you see that I'm busy?"

The children pull even harder in response to her

annoyance.

"Can you take us to see the party? We want to see the party!"

Chett is not entirely in the mood to go to some rowdy event after a long day of selling newspapers and magazines under the scorching sun on the busy street of Norodom Boulevard, where passing cars and motorbikes continuously honk at her to move out of the way. The maddening sound of the beeping and tooting that she has heard every day for the last three years of her life fills her ears, causing her forehead to tighten as she imagines what it would be like to be near the loud party tent. The pain in her head causes her to shake and her teeth to chatter. She is too physically and mentally depleted to do anything but lie down and sleep.

But when she looks down at the pleading faces of her siblings, a pang of sympathy hits her as she remembers how excited and happy they were just a few moments ago. She cannot afford to take any happiness away from them when this is all she can offer besides love and affection. Fighting back the pain in her head, she exhales and agrees to take the children out to the event.

With Kheang's hand in hers and Pheak comfortably resting on her right hip, scrawny legs dangling like twigs, Chett exits the alley and approaches a pink tent that is positioned in the middle of the street. She slowly draws closer while still keeping some distance from the tent. She can see a bunch of tables and chairs occupied with people dressed in bright, colorful clothes. Chett doesn't dare go any closer, secretly admiring the beauty of the event from afar.

Gorgeous women in stunning, sparkly dresses that glimmer against the colorful background lights sit gracefully around one table, talking and giggling in utter delight. The entire block echoes with glee and laughter, filling the children's hearts with happiness and worry for fear of getting caught watching the event.

Chett stands still, taking in the magnificence of the occasion, when suddenly she realizes Kheang has gotten

28   *Modern Literature of Cambodia*

loose of her grip and is running toward the party tent. Chett quickly rushes after the little boy and grabs him by the arm before he enters the party. Kheang tries to break free as Chett struggles to pull him back.

"Get off of me! I want to dance! Let go of me!"

With tired limbs and a toddler on her hip, Chett is not strong enough to stop her stubborn little brother. Kheang once again escapes and charges into the party tent through the entrance foyer. Chett runs in after, hoping to catch up to him and drag him back home before he causes any trouble.

The inside of the tent feels strange to her even though she is only standing by the entrance. A sense of disparity fills her as she looks at the world before her. She has transitioned into a whole new realm of reality with just one step. She turns around and looks far away at the route she has taken to get here. She sees nothing but a dirty narrow street with puddles here and there that reflect a dark ocean with stars above and the white decrepit buildings that are home to criminals and prostitutes, piled with trash on either side. The street is illuminated by some dim orange street lights that cannot even guide her all the way back to where she actually belongs — a wrecked home in a dark alley. She turns around to face the magic world and finds herself staring at a much smaller and more orderly domain than her own. This world is one where people dance and laugh as if they know nothing about the existence of hunger and sorrow.

The people look even more exotic close up. Men in clean, light shirts and dark trousers with their hair properly combed, slightly bounce to the tempo of the music as they spread their arms out to dance behind beautiful women dressed in flamboyant, shimmering dresses and high heels, their shiny hair bundled up in buns or side curls that perfectly compliment their full faces with blushed cheeks and rich red lips. She sees a group of children dancing playfully on one side of the dance floor. Among them she spots a girl about her age in a pink fluffy dress, dancing with a cheerful smile that spreads from ear to ear across her satisfied tiny face— the smile of a promising future.

Chett looks at her three-year-old sister who is resting securely in her weak and shaky arms, gazing blindly at the lights with big round innocent eyes, not knowing what will become of their future. Everything in this alien world is hopeful and prosperous. She wants to belong here instead of the world with a drunken father who could care less about his children and is never home to provide them with the love and warmth they need.

In the mist of the crowd, Chett suddenly sees Kheang dashing towards her in tears followed by a man pointing his forefinger at her face ordering them to leave. They hurriedly scramble out of the tent to find a dry corner somewhere on the street where Chett comforts the terrified little boy.

Trembling with fear, Kheang quietly murmurs, "I only wanted to dance. I thought they would let me; they all seemed very nice."

Chett wraps her free arm even tighter around her fragile little brother and says, "Everyone seems nice. The whole world seems nice if you don't look too carefully."

Taking her brother's right hand in hers and with little Pheak quietly asleep on her right hip, Chett begins to make their way back to where they belong, leaving behind the world of ringing, cheerful sounds of happiness that the three had just experienced.

.   .   .   .

With Kheang and Pheak soundly asleep, Chett thinks of the children's faces she saw earlier. She can still hear their echoing laughter as they danced. What she remembers most clearly, though, is the girl in the pink dress. Chett can recall her face with faint, red blushed cheeks and hair so long and glossy that it ran down her back slightly touching her butt as she elegantly moved to the rhythm of the music. Chett can't help but wonder what differentiates her and the girl in the pink dress? They are both girls. They

30   *Modern Literature of Cambodia*

are probably even the same age, and they live in the same neighborhood. But why is it that the two girls belong in such different worlds?

With the party music still playing loud and sharp, Chett gets up and imitates the way the girl in the pink dress danced. She stands with her back straight, strutting with arms out, bent at the elbows with her wrists and fingers splayed back, and leaning her head from side to side as she moves rhythmically to the music. She starts moving around the room and finds herself standing in front of a cracked mirror hanging on the damp wall of her home. She puts her arms down and examines herself carefully. Now she clearly realizes the answer to her question. Her dirty face is framed with messy strands of hair falling awkwardly to shoulders draped with a patched, long sleeve shirt exposing a dusty pair of hands that tremble from lack of nutrition. This makes it very clear that, even though the girls are the same, they are completely different.

Chett turns away shamefully and returns to the corner where her siblings peacefully sleep with their backs against each other and joins them. She closes her eyes as the feelings of shame and inferiority well up through her throat and pour out as tears. She soon falls heavily asleep from today's weariness that is already prepared and waiting to challenge her once again when she opens her eyes tomorrow.

Girl in a Pink Dress (2)

She opens the glass door to an air-conditioned restaurant where table after table of friends and families gather to eat a traditional Cambodian breakfast of hot noodle soup. The greasy smell of fried minced garlic in chicken broth soup, mixed with the floral fragrance of tea and the soothing scent of freshly brewed coffee, lingers in the air filling her nose with delight as she inhales. Like every other day of her life, the thought of savoring that hot soup, complete with a tinge of fresh lime, makes her mouth water and her tummy grumble. The sharp clatter of spoons against the ceramic bowls and the slurping of noodles and soup are all so familiar to Pha's ears as she glances over the many groups of diners before her.

Some are vigorously dipping pieces of meat in chili sauce and jamming noodles into their mouths, while others are busily talking to friends over steaming cups of coffee and tea awaiting their fresh and healthy breakfast soup. Pha looks around for a table she could go to.

She then approaches a nearby table where a man sits by himself. "Are you interested in buying a newspaper, sir?" she asks as she holds one up before her. The man casually reads the headlines on the front page. His face shows no interest. He shakes his head "no" and continues sipping his tea.

Pha moves to another table where a middle-aged woman sits with her daughter. She holds up a magazine and asks, "Would you like one, miss?"

The woman takes the magazine from her hand at the sight of the latest celebrity gossip on the cover and flicks through the pages with great interest. While she browses through the magazine, Pha stealthily looks over at the woman's daughter.

The girl is about her height. The two even look about the same age. And they both have dark, medium-length hair. The only difference, though, is that the daughter, neatly clothed in a pink fluffy dress, is sitting in a comfy chair with her chicken-broth noodle soup placed before her while Pha,

32   *Modern Literature of Cambodia*

dressed in old worn-out clothes that are covered in blotches of dirt here and there, is standing with an empty stomach.

Pha watches the girl with strong envy and great admiration for her beauty. She continues to watch as the girl in the pink dress picks up her spoon and chopsticks.

Pha cannot help but salivate as the girl puts the noodles in her mouth. Pha swallows her saliva as the girl swallows her soup and can almost taste the peppery chicken noodle goodness as she glimpses the pieces of meat floating in the girl's bowl.

The girl in the pink dress suddenly complains with irritation after tasting her soup and whines about not having gone to her favorite restaurant to eat what she wants. She pushes the bowl away, kicks her feet under the table, and cries with anger and frustration. Her mother returns the magazine, waves her hand at Pha, which suggests that she is not interested in buying it.

She then turns to her daughter and says, "My poor baby, I am so sorry. I promise we will go there tomorrow, okay?" The daughter smiles and quickly nods with satisfaction.

Pha throws the girl in the pink dress one last distasteful glance and walks away with her newspapers, magazines, and empty stomach.

6

NOCH Sakona was an official in the Ministry of the Interior at the time he won the first place prize in short fiction for this story in the 2007 Nou Hach Literary Award competition. He has some unpublished poems and a collection of stories "Kapsok Village" that apologizes for the past. The theme of "improvement" in the story below represents one type of modern Cambodian fiction that focuses on "development."

Season's End for a Lady of the Night
Noch Sakona

A man with salt and pepper hair turns to look at the door to his room as it slowly opens. He sees a beautiful young girl about seventeen years old. The burly man who had opened the door bows his head to someone outside then pulls the door shut leaving her inside.

Then the man in the room turns down the T.V. and examines her as she walks toward him lying on the bed. And he asks her a question: "What did that man tell you?"

"He told me to give you a massage."

"A regular or erotic massage?"

She doesn't reply, just smiles. He tells her to go take a shower. She goes into the bathroom and shuts the door, thinking: *Why is life so bad like this. My customers are always older men with greying hair. Is this guy a tiger or a wolf? It doesn't matter since they buy me either way.*

Then she leaves the bathroom and walks over to the bed again. She turns her face to him, thinking: *Isn't this wrong. He will probably ask me to take off my clothes so he can lustfully examine my body.*

34   *Modern Literature of Cambodia*

While she is thinking this, the customer asks her to open his suitcase. It is full of sexy negligees. She wonders what's going on, they are so beautiful and lovely. *Why is he acting like this. I don't understand....*

She picks up a negligee and holds it up. The man seems to understand how she feels and says: "You can select any one you want."

"Okay, thanks."

"Just try it on," the man responds.

She happily tries it on, saying: "This is becoming a strange evening. You are different from the other men."

The man, who seems interested in her, says: "You are good at selecting a negligee that compliments your figure. Someone sent all these to my daughter. There are too many for her to wear so you can take some."

Looking in admiration at herself in the negligee, she responds: "Thank you! But...what should I do for you, uncle?"

He smiles, asking: "Why do you call me uncle?"

"What do you want me to call you other than uncle? Do you want me to act like the girls you had before?"

He smiles and asks her to take out the oil used to reduce muscle pain. And she gives him a body massage. The man thinks to himself: *She's not as skillful as the previous girls.*

Then he asks her: "Where did you learn this type of massage?"

"It's how I used to massage my mother and grandmother...I never went to massage school." How she speaks indicates to him that she is an honest girl, but he thinks she probably has a lot of secrets.

As she gives him the massage, she keeps thinking about his behavior—he doesn't want sex, but instead asks her a lot of questions related to her past—as she thinks that prostitutes also need some romance.

She tells him about her life—

"I am a farmer's daughter. When I was growing up, I asked about him, but got no answer. And t made my mother cry. She told me my father died when I was little... on the battlefield. Every morning my mother would go work for other people and was never home. At that time, my brother and I didn't understand the difficulties she endured; we just cried because we were hungry. Every evening we would have dinner together; but never any delicious food, just enough to be full.

When I grew up, I helped my mother. I would earn money to buy rice. When my brother was old enough to go to school, my mother sent him to an organization that helps children.

Time passed and I grew to be a woman. I felt that our poor life made us both miserable, but we had no choice other than trying to survive. One evening after we had dinner, we went to sleep early without even caring about watching a movie like we usually did at a neighbor's house. My mother had a persistent cough, sometimes even coughing up blood. I felt so sorry for her, but she would reply: 'I'm fine, I'm not falling down; I'm just working too hard so it makes me feel like this. I'll go rest a bit and I'll be better. Don't worry.'

We were struggling to survive. And my mother became thinner and thinner. She could not sleep, and we didn't have enough food. One night I saw my mother crying with tears flowing into her sunken cheeks. I felt so sorry for her. These tears were the sign of my mother's pain living in such a miserable condition unable to help her daughter. And that night, my mother asked a lady for help."

After she finished telling this much of her story, the man asked: "At that time wasn't there any organization to give you advice?"

"Yes, there was, someone from a religious organization. They gave hope to my mother to think of God who lives in paradise; he keeps all those suffering beings in his heart."

The man keeps asking questions about her life.

She replies: "That auntie took me to live with her. She took me some place where I saw a lot of older girls wearing

36   *Modern Literature of Cambodia*

makeup and new dresses. The owner welcomed my mother and let her sit in an air-conditioned room. I don't know what my mother understood but she seemed to feel more confident. The lady looked me up and down then asked: 'How old are you? Come closer to me...'.

'Sixteen,' I replied without moving closer.

She smiled, nodding her head and said: 'I feel so sorry for you...you can help me by working here; I will treat you well.'

That lady was attractive and well dressed, but we left there without having lunch with her. My mother and I ate lunch and talked. She gave me a lot of advice since she was worried about me: 'I'll be going back home this evening. Be sure to serve this woman well and do as she asks! Looking at her, I think she is kind...'.

I saw tears forming in my mother's eyes then fall onto the plate. We will be eating a meal of tears. I feel like crying too and speak to my mother: 'I want to return with you. We can be dishwashers at a noodle shop or hired labor in the rice fields.'

My mother shakes her head and speaks with difficulty trying not to cry: 'No. You feel pity for me no matter whether our life improves a bit or not, we are still at the level of servants. Stay here and be strong. I pray to the Buddha for your good luck.'"

After she finished this much of her story, the man seems shocked and asks her: "You never saw your mother after that?"

"That's right. I never saw her after that separation. I started living with that lady who asked me to call her 'mother' as if I were her real daughter. She taught me how to do housework, how to behave with correct manners at social functions. She bought me beautiful clothes and makeup, taught me how to sing, and how to speak eloquently. A few months later, my skin turned whiter from treatments and everyone became jealous of me because that lady treated me so well."

"Season's End for a Lady of the Night"   37

"Did you like it?" The man asked.

"No. My life became like a bird in a cage. Her kindness to me was so strange. One day when I told her I wanted to visit my mother, she told me my mother had died from a blood disease. When I heard this, I felt lifeless, covered my face and cried. There was no benefit to this new life, but I had no choice.

Periodically, I saw the lady's husband when he came to visit her. He was the head of the army. Another girl there, told me that the owner of this house was his second wife.

One day, I carried the beverages to the guests, including a guest who was quite old. She introduced me to him explaining that I was her youngest daughter. I felt so shy when he glanced at me and answered his questions with uncomfortable hesitation."

The customer with the salt-and-pepper hair then asked: "That old man was rich?"

"Yes. He gave me 100 dollars like it was 100 riel. I didn't want it but she insisted that I take it. I had to turn it over to her."

The girl stopped speaking, because she was tired from talking while giving him a massage. But he still wanted to know more about her life and asked her about her first love.

She replied hesitantly. "One day I went to Sihanoukville and I stayed in a nice villa. That night I had dinner with the lady and that old man I'd met before. The lady called him 'Excellency.' And then he poured some red wine for the lady and she selected his food. If an outsider were viewing this scene, it would appear like a regular family: mother, father, and daughter. But it was so sad for a girl like me without any life experience. I was like an animal force-fed until grown and then slaughtered.

Then I became woozy from the alcohol. This is difficult to explain. The lady took me to a bedroom and I heard the sound of her whispering: 'Sleep now. Good luck and happiness will be yours because that old guy has everything, including a lot of money. I'm cheering you on.'

38   *Modern Literature of Cambodia*

My body felt as soft as cotton as the old man coldly caressed me. Money destroyed my virginity. Afterwards the lady comforted me saying: 'It's over now. You didn't lose anything. I will have some jewelry made for you. You have to understand that in this society, you have to be smart. You can't be honest all the time.'

What she said made me think of is everything that she had done to me. Everything she did was insincere. She destroyed my whole life. Since that day, I've tried to see through the falsehoods in this presentation of a beautiful world without mercy. This is the story of my 'first love'."

The guy with the salt and pepper hair wanted to comfort her as she continued to tell her story.

"I decided from that time to smile, flirting with my destiny in order to overcome it. This is the best way, however unjust, for me to win. I'm still meeting that old guy, and I'm still a slave to my customer's passion, however distasteful...".

After finishing her story, she stopped the massage and lay down next to him, saying: "Now I'll sleep with you. You are a nice old guy who makes me feel happy. You are not as bad as the other men. You ask me questions to make me feel better." She kisses him.

He looks at her and realizes she just wants someone to comfort her. So he stops and rubs away a tear from beneath her eye and says: "But I understand that your tears don't indicate a solution; you continue to deceive yourself. If you keep crying, how can I help you?"

Before he finishes speaking, she puts her hand over his mouth to silence him: "I cry because I am so deeply hurt beyond words because no one helps me...". She's weeping as she speaks. Now she is on top of him. He pats her on the back and pushes her off.

"My poor girl. Your face shows how much you're emotionally hurt. So much pain that you may shatter." He comforts her again. "Sometimes destiny can lead to a blessing. You're still young. You don't know much about life. If I told you that during the Sihanouk era his Excellency's wife was originally a prostitute, then you wouldn't believe me. You should understand that there is no night without day, no rain without sunshine... so! I heard that you can sing. I want to listen to you. Which song do you like?"

She wiped away her tears and smiled, laughing and crying at the same time. Then she replied: "I don't prefer any specific song; I can sing any song for my customer." As she is speaking, he turns on the karaoke machine, saying: "Do you know how to sing: 'Missing You' or 'Last Night You Were with Me'?"

"Yes, of course. But don't laugh at me since I might not be that great." Her resonant voice showed that she had talent. And he thought that she was like a diamond concealed in stone or a beautiful flower uncovered in some deep forest. Such a miserable girl, he thinks: *Either I help you or I overlook your suffering.*

When she finished singing, he smiled to encourage her. And she thought if there weren't night girls like her how could there be "good" girls. He asked that poor girl about the dark side of her life.

And she replied: "Actually, this kind of life is not my choice. It just happened, and it has been painful. I used to think about how I could escape from this, but I couldn't find a way out. Consider it from my perspective, if you were a girl like me, which would you choose: the night girl or the precious girl? If I'm not wrong, you appear to be some kind of official with a lot of money, and you could buy a young girl the same age as your daughter to satisfy your sexual needs. The difference is you would never do this to your own daughter. On the radio, I heard positive things about women such as 'women are the mothers of the nation' to raise awareness about gender or to demand a woman's right to be a leader. I ask you if the term 'precious girl' can be used only for a good wife or some woman to promote? I only hear the word prostitute or night-girl or sex worker to describe me. And sometimes I'm used as the object for everyone's concern

40   *Modern Literature of Cambodia*

about condom use. Rather than just saying 'precious girl' that gives value to all women, have they ever thought about the real solution to this problem, or helped us escape this reality? Are the tears of a prostitute less painful or the speech from a girl like me less worthy than one from an honorable woman? Goodness. Last night what were you waiting for. I know what I'm doing and I also need some rest." She said crying again.

The guy thought about this and replied: "I understand about this kind of life. I discovered your talent and now I'm thinking about how I could help you."

Having said this, he gave her his business card. She accepted it thinking that he was the strangest man she had ever met. She examined his name and position seeing that he was the director of an NGO that opposed prostitution. She felt happy about this but then felt badly about her comment that all men are the same. And she apologized to him.

He comforted her again and spoke: "Do you know that today female academics try to promote women in leadership positions not only in the National Institute but also in NGOs. They try to promote justice for woman. I have a plan to save sex workers by changing their lives so they can become 'mothers of the nation.' I've established a center called Phum Srei Prohsav. Miserable girls get training there and acquire a skill."

After he finished, the girl said: "You are so kind! I want to see that kind of example. I hope your plan succeeds."

"With effort anyone can succeed. You could too. You should be proud of yourself."

The poor girl woke up from her misery. She looked at his face and said: "What can I call you?"

"You can refer to me in many ways. Think of an appropriate term for my age."

When she heard this, she trembled and asked: "Father! Can I call you father?" I'm a poor girl without parents, can I? Or do you mind since I'm a girl of no value? Can I beg for your mercy?"

"Daughter," he said "of course it doesn't hurt unless

also afraid of the teacher asking for money; afraid of his yelling and screaming; afraid of his painful pinching of my arms and stomach. I'm afraid he will throw away my books and whiteboard marker. I'm even afraid of the lesson guidelines I have to buy. I'm just afraid, afraid, afraid, because I'm the poorest student in the class and at the very bottom of the class rankings. During study time, the teacher's loud outbursts remind me of landmine explosions. Trembling, I feel terrified in class.

I've never been to the after-school sessions (which cost extra money). One day when I walked over to that class-room, I unexpectedly heard a softer voice from my teacher— "Children, children"—speaking so nicely to every child. Nothing more to say; I just started feeling badly about this. I feel so pessimistic about education at my public school. Nothing can change my mind about this no matter what. There is no way to change my opinion; this pessimism is so deeply rooted in my mind.

Our teacher is supposed to be our second mother, but this one demands money from students. So this second mother is the one who extorts money. A real mother provides money for school or snacks.

I don't blame anyone for this problem. And I don't really hate or get angry with my teacher. If I think clearly about this situation again, I will admit that a teacher has responsibilities. If my teacher didn't ask for money, how could he support himself on such a low salary? He would die. His salary is only equal to the amount a high ranking official spends for just one night drinking at a bar. The more I think about this, the more confused I get. I think it over repeatedly and so many issues arise. I can't think of any solution. I feel hopeless about my future studies. I begin to act differently and I start skipping classes. I become a delinquent student.

This year I have decided to retake this grade level because of how many absences I have even though I didn't fail the work. I went to the administration office before the term exam because they announced how many absences I

44   *Modern Literature of Cambodia*

had. I thought they might "go easy" on me for this, and "going easy" is positive. If there is any student who cannot pass the exam or has too many absences, they can negotiate "going easy" at the office. When I studied in class, I never went to the administration office; but this time I have the honor of going there to meet the teacher who controls my class. We talk seriously….

"Pay the same as everyone else. Don't be different," he tells me. I'm stunned and feel so disappointed about what he's said.

I still try to respond: "Teacher, I'm an impoverished student. Please help me just this once."

Suddenly he blames me: "If you can't help yourself, how can I help you? Just go! Don't mess with me! Just pay me fifty percent of the usual amount because you are poor."

I began to beg him for some compassion: "Teacher, is there any other choice? Can I ask to take the exam again? The reason I skip class is I don't have money to pay all the extra fees so I go to the library or the debate club on literature instead. That's why I have so many absences. Teacher, please take pity on me. I'm an impoverished student," I said respectfully in a polite tone. This time I felt like a target for the teacher's blame.

The teacher said: "If I pity you, my stomach goes hungry. It's your class time but you skip it and go to the library." My teacher spoke rudely while looking at his watch. And he turned to his computer monitor, which was full of games.

Even though I felt angry with my teacher, I still remained polite and respectful, and I said goodbye: "Thanks so much teacher. I would like to say goodbye."

And the teacher did not bother to respond.

I left the room, feeling so hopeless. I smiled while shaking my head about what my teacher had just done to me. I walked over to my old bicycle and rode back home.

On the way, the road was very crowded with cars whose exhaust polluted the environment. I think and imagine your own body bleeds. But to be human, we must be embarrassed of our situation and not waste time in changing it. I encourage you, daughter. The past is like a torn skirt, you are not as bad as some academics say. They create a virus or a nuclear bomb to destroy people. We should change the season to a new one. You must have hope..."

Translated by Teri Yamada and NHIM Soknea

7

HENG Oudom was born in 1992 in Kompong Cham province. He received the second place prize for short fiction in the 2011 Nou Hach Literary Awards competition for "I Repeat a Level." At that time he was a law student at the Royal University of Law and Economics, while working as a free-lance reporter for various magazines. He has received awards for his creative writing from Oxfam and other organizations. In 2015 the Ministry of Education finally implemented reforms to stop rampant cheating on the national examinations but public school teachers remain seriously underpaid.

I Repeat a Level
Heng Oudom

I am the kind of person no one notices. If the truth were told, others view me like useless dust. Sometimes it's not just one person but everyone who despises me. Even those in society and school dislike me. My relatives hate me even more. Also my classmates, they don't like me because I'm different. I don't go along with the others; I just don't get along. In conclusion, I don't adhere to the Cambodian proverb: "Follow the course of the river."

Everyone sees a lazy student when they observe my demeanor. I feel negative about education. In my opinion, school is not a place of learning. It's just a marketplace for business. Moreover, I know that the classroom is like a jail for criminals. Every time I step into a classroom, I begin to feel badly. I feel faint, get a headache, and become scared, waiting for the money-collector to solicit my payment. I am a lot; it seems like I am a foolish person.

If I ask my parents for money, they would surely give it to me and I could move on to the next level; but I can't do that! I can't pour pure water into a polluted sea. If I pour the water and expect it to counter the corruption, it certainly won't work. So I need to eliminate all the corruption, and I must start with myself.

If other people don't obey the traffic laws, it is their business; the important thing is that I respect myself. I provide my own dignity. If I give money to the teacher, no one else will know; but I will, so I just can't do it. My conscience would bother me if I didn't do the right thing. I'm happy to accept this injustice in others but not in myself, following Socrates' example.

I've known many teachers who talk about how difficult their lives are as teachers. When I hear this, I really want to become a teacher and I've already set my goal. If I become a teacher, I will eliminate the corruption in the education sector starting with me. Whatever other people think about me, if I become a teacher, I won't accept any bribes because I want the education system to become better and bring better human resources into teaching. Now I cannot bribe my teacher. I want to be a good educator so I need to educate my conscience and myself. I'm not happy that all those around me are hungry. Whatever I do, I expect a humble life so I don't want anything. To just survive, I don't need to demand money from my students. I still can live with my ability and real knowledge. I will try to do my duty to the nation. I don't need to be rich besides just doing my job. So I can do the right thing. I will try my best to perform my work according to my conscience….

．　　　．　　　．　　　．

Two years later, I have discovered a quiet place to escape from the scariness of school and the voice of my teacher. I rarely go to school. I study less in the classroom,

46   *Modern Literature of Cambodia*

about two or three days a week, and sometimes I never go at all. I became a delinquent student who studies outside of class. I go to the library during study time and this has become my habit. This is also the reason that the teacher feels unhappy with me. It is also the main reason that I repeated the same level again last year. I began to discover knowledge by myself, and I started to write and read a lot of books.

I hold imaginary discussions with the scholars whose books I read published in both Cambodia and outside the country. I also met well-educated people in the library. One day I submitted my work to the school's poetry and short story contest. My submission was accepted although no one realized I had written it. No one realized that I was the top pick. Even my teacher and my classmates, who used to sit next to me, never realized this until the principal announced my name. Then they knew and realized that I could survive with my integrity in spite of their corruption....

Translated by Teri Yamada and NHIM Soknea

8

SUN Try was born on August 23, 1987, in Siem Reap. He has a BA in Cambodian Literature from the Royal University of Phnom Penh and was working on an MA in Linguistics there in 2013 while serving as an official in the Ministry of Rural Development in Kandal Province. He has also published children's stories and received an award for children's fiction from the organization Room to Read. The two following stories were awarded the third place prize for fiction in the 2013 Nou Hach Literary Competition.

Exhibition Year 3333
Sun Try

It's midnight. Fake sunlight appears, illuminating everything as clear as glass. Everyone is driving sky cars to the highest hotel, level with the clouds. In that hotel there are many millionaires from around the world bidding on an exotic plant, the last one in the world. We are proud of Cambodia because we are winning the bid for this valuable plant. A millionaire from Angkor is successful in the highest bid. Cambodians are surprised and want to see this plant. Some people fly from the ground; others drive from other planets and land in the Kingdom of Cambodia.

When the millionaire arrives home, he plants it in his garden and sells tickets to tourists for its exhibition. I, Sun Try, also bought a ticket for 100 million riel to see this plant.

Gosh! What a wonderful plant. It has a purple flower and a wonderful fragrance. "Sir, can you tell me the name of

48   *Modern Literature of Cambodia*

this flower?"

The millionaire whispered to me because he didn't want anyone else to hear: "This is called the Mhamom, which Cambodians used a thousand years ago as a common spice for soup...".

"This is a real story"

Translated by Teri Shaffer Yamada and NHIM Soknea, 2013

9

Becoming Young Again
Sun Try

There was a little boy who lived by a coconut palm—with its fronds, coconuts, and flowers—which produced delicious coconut milk. When he was little, the boy always played under this palm tree. He would pull a frond down and tug off a coconut for some delicious food that he happily ate. As time passed, the little boy grew up and left the palm tree.

Once in a while, he would return to visit this coconut palm tree. When it noticed him coming, the palm tree seemed very happy and said: "The little boy has come back to live with me! We can play again and you can take care of me, watering and clearing the ground."

The little boy, now grown up, answered: "No! I've come here only for your sweet coconut milk." And as soon as he finished the coconut milk, he left.

Some time later, the young man returned to the palm tree, which was still so happy to see him, saying: "Little boy, have you come back to live with me?"

He replied: "No, I need to sell your coconuts so I can have enough money to get married."

The palm tree answered: "You can cut my fronds and coconuts to take them for sale."

As soon as the young man sold everything, he stayed away from the palm tree until it had grown very old. And then the little boy, now a mature man, returned again. As soon as the palm tree saw him, it became very happy and spoke to him like before. But the man said: "No! This time I need help building my house. I need your fronds for my roof and your trunk for the beam."

50   *Modern Literature of Cambodia*

The palm tree agreed to let the man, once that little boy, cut it down and do with its remains as he wished.

.   .   .   .

Time passes like water flowing from the Sivalingas in the Kulen Mountains down to the Siem Reap River. In the end, the water flows into the great Tonlesap Lake and we never seeing it flowing back again.   We can see the former little boy, now an old man, hugging his knees in the pouring rain near the old stump of a coconut palm tree.

A holy man appears and asks him: "What do you want now?"

"I want to be young again."

Translated by Teri Shaffer Yamada and NHIM Soknea, 2013

10

CHIEB Kim Heang received the first place prize for short fiction in the 2009 Nou Hach Literary Awards competition for his story "Starlight." It is unusual for its transnational theme, in this case Cambodia and France, and its discussion of the environment and Buddhism.

Starlight
Chieb Kim Heang

Steung Mean Chey, my wonderland…. The pile of garbage is my property; the property that never drains dry.

My name is Chey. I do not know why I ended up living here or even when I arrived. Nor do I know my age. My background is also a mystery.

Every day I compete with others to pick up things that were thrown away on the stinking garbage pile.

Many people run after the garbage truck. Garbage is our money; others and I run after the money. Some people say that I have done this job even in my previous life. How could they know about my previous life? I don't even know about my own background now. I don't even know my parents.

One day there is an accident. A monk is thrown into a fetid water channel with a dead dog in it. The people don't dare to help the monk; they just stand and watch as I save him from the smelly water. The awful odor is easy for me. Still it doesn't mean I don't like the fragrance of flowers. I know that rotting things attract flies; flowers attract butterflies. There is no butterfly on the garbage heap. It has only flies, blue and

52   *Modern Literature of Cambodia*

grey headed flies.

Gold is still gold even when it has fallen into the mud. The monk has fallen into smelly water; no one dares to approach him since he is not gold. The value of a person is based on the situation. I help him to his home in the pagoda.

People come to offer provisions to the monk but no one shows concern for me.

The monk still suffers from this unbelievable accident. He says to me, "Thank you so much! You don't have any parents so stay with me. It is better than living on the garbage heap. If you stay there you live with your karma. If you stay here, you live with sages. I need someone to stay and assist me since I am old."

I start my new life as a pagoda boy. It is different from living on the garbage mountain. I learn how to respect other people properly, how to respect the Buddha, how to speak skillfully, how to calm my temper. I learn about morality and apply it to myself. My daily work is to fill the water jar, prepare incense sticks and candles, clean and organize the room, and so forth.

The monk I live with is great. He blesses water; scares ghosts away; brings good luck to people and other things. He can also tell fortunes, predicting what will happen in the future.

I live happily with him because he can help me if I encounter bad luck.

But I wonder, if he really is so wonderful, why couldn't he prevent that accident? This question keeps bothering me; I don't have an answer.

The monk never tells me that he can earn a lot of money because he knows magic. He helps students pass exams; he increases the business of his supporters; he cures diseases, and does other things. He is so famous. Even Cambodians living in France, the United States, and Australia invite him to bless them.

He gets an invitation to France. One month before his departure, he learns some new Dharma and practices some actions to make his supporters feel trust and confidence in him. He says the people over there are so smart he has to create some activity to make them believe in him.

He practices many times like a dancer practicing before a performance. He practices speaking louder, stronger, with proper words. He practices blessing the water, throwing fruits to bless the supporters, and making noise to scare ghosts away.

He receives his travel itinerary. According to it, he will be too busy even to take a city tour.

My monk wants money to repair the temple because in Cambodia people are deeply impressed with pagoda complexes that have a big temple. Many people will come then.

He is so happy. He wants to see France. Some people say France is like a paradise. He has never been to paradise; just seen pictures on the walls of the pagoda.

One student living in the same pagoda even tells me that people used to say that paradise was located on the moon. When the astronauts arrived on the moon, they said nothing about finding paradise there.

Grandpa monk always shows me a picture of the Buddha who comes from paradise by an emerald stairway. In Laos, there was an old pagoda that had a picture of Buddha coming from paradise by a bamboo stair.

"Chey, I feel sorry that I'm going to France in my old age. It would have been better to go abroad when I was young. I will bring you there if we have a chance. I will bring you to see how they live, to see smart people who can make guns, electronic machines, and manage Cambodia for nearly a century."

The monk continues talking to me, "If there are many uneducated people in Cambodia like you, we will be defeated. I don't want you to rely on luck. You have to study, to be educated."

He continues, "I became a monk when I was young. I

54   *Modern Literature of Cambodia*

knew nothing about monks. My mother brought me to the pagoda because our family was poor. She took me to be educated, to have a better life, but I did not get any skill besides respecting the Buddha and learning how to perform blessings. There is no angel to help me and I can't help Buddhists. I can teach you, but I know little. There are many understanding people. You should find them and listen to them to find the right way in your life. You have to study; you have to learn to become smart; you have to be strong; you have to think more deeply and widely ...this is the similar to the Pope's advice when he instructs his followers."

The old monk has started on his journey to France. He hasn't forgotten to bring various magical items but has also packed modern medicines.

After he arrives, he tells me about being scared because the plane is in the sky not on the ground. He talks about the plane flying across the open sea and how he is afraid it would crash with the angels. His plane is on time having traversed many countries. Cambodians living in France come to welcome him at Charles de Gaul airport. Planes are taking off one a minute. The French unlike Cambodians do not need to learn magic to fly; they produce planes that can carry people in the sky.

Along the way from the airport, he watches the passing scenery, thinking about what he sees. There are a lot of vehicles and high buildings. He wonders why Cambodians living in France are so afraid? What are they afraid of? Perhaps they are afraid of something they can't see such as ghosts or hell...does hell really exist? In France, there are doctors and specialists. Their soldiers are strong. France is great to produce a nuclear bomb. Is there anything greater than nuclear power?

The French have different beliefs from Cambodians and they instruct their people differently. Their point of view must be correct, which is why they could colonize Indochina before World War II.

He experiences many questions arising in his mind for which he has no answers.

He tells me that he goes to bless one Cambodian family living not far from the nuclear power plant. He is afraid it might explode and scared that the power of his magic might not protect him. He has never used his magic in this kind of circumstance before.

He tells me that the owner of the house thanks him saying, "I would like to express great appreciation to you for coming so far to bless us, ensuring a happy life." After he hears this, he feels ashamed.

He tells me that if there were a meteor, Cambodians would be afraid, believing it to be a sign of impending war, a sign from the gods. In France, they would not be surprised by this kind of event. They would announce its coming appearance on the news broadcast to everyone. They would tell people it could be viewed from two to four a.m. in the western part of the sky. They'd also explain its physical composition and that a U.S. astronaut had recorded and touched it.

"I have to change," he says.

He stays one month in France; it is so short. He thinks that if he could go there again, he would take time to go around the city to study how people live and other things.

"It could develop our ideas," that follower of the Buddha tells me. He says that he does not know whether it is right or wrong to be a monk. Some monks or Buddhists do not lie because they want to go to heaven. "But A Chey," he says, "We have to die first. I don't want to become a Buddha since no one could be like him."

He continues his thoughts, "Some people respect cows as a god. If someone eats beef, they will be punished. Europeans eat beef because it gives them strength. Some people do not eat pork, but it is a Chinese super meat. I never teach people not to kill animals; I also eat meat. I don't know whom to follow. We are Cambodians; we say our culture is great. We are Buddhists so Buddhism is the best religion. But other nations, they claim that they are great too. Even a servant declares he is better than his boss. This is the human condition."

I think he has become more understanding since returning from France. He seems stronger, more active, self-determined and reasonable. He states that no country is better than our homeland although the weather elsewhere might be better; Cambodia is the paradise of our soul.

"A Chey," he says to me "next year I will take you to France. You have to study to become famous. Your future depends on your attitude. You have to go to school to obtain knowledge. You have to remember that we live in the world, everyone is our friend. We have to help each other; we must not look down on anyone, even the poor."

He teaches me, "We are born as humans. We will be happy if we are born rich. If we are born in a poor family, we will be sad. No one can see what tomorrow will bring so we have to take care of today. If we want a sharp knife, we have to use it often. Knowledge is like a sharp knife used to solve problems in our life. Some define life as suffering; some say life is basically happy; others say life is hard work. How we should live as humans must be through striving hard for success."

He continues with further instruction. "One person can live about twenty thousand days. People need to eat, sleep, breathe; they need both physical and mental security. They need friends. They need interaction and so forth. They need money, fame, love and health. We are in charge of our own lives; we are our own bosses. Therefore, you have to think about finding your own way. A Chey, you may not be able to go to school but at least you must know how to read and write. You have to speak skillfully and politely to everyone, especially to older people. You have to learn a variety of skills including a foreign language. You have to develop your ability. You have to be opened-mind to accept another person's criticism. You can raise chickens, ducks, and pigs to sell for money. Or you can farm...don't be afraid of punishment in the next life. Only the rich should be afraid of the next life because they don't know whether they will be rich again. It is better to live on a river that contains fish than on a garbage mountain. We are poor not because of punishment from a previous life but because we are not well educated. Cambodians care only about the future not the present. We are Cambodians; we have to love and help each other. We must band together then our country will be developed like the Khmer empire in the past."

And I responded, "I promise I will. Believe me!"

Translated by PHOU Chakriya

11

The following story by RY Sarong won the third place prize for short fiction in the 2015 Nou Hach Literary Awards competition. It is particularly interesting because of its treatment of the environment.

Ghost Environment
Ry Sarong

"'Environment' means 'everything around us'." I suddenly remembered this definition. And I thought critically about it since I'd wandered into a very strange place. I looked around at the environment, feeling sad. I wondered how these people could live in such a dirty place?

After looking around, I realized that all life here was seriously threatened by environmental contaminants. When the wind blew periodically, there would be a horrendous stench like decomposing corpses.

I kept moving forward nervously, while observing many people going in and out of the area. Everyone looked horrible. Some people had no arms; others, no legs; and still others had only heads. Some were very skinny with ratty hair and oozing lesions on their bodies.

Looking in another direction, I saw a man with a huge, swollen belly but with rib bones still visible and liquor bottles along with snack bags hanging from his waist belt. I walked toward him and asked: "Uncle! What is this village called? Why is the place so dirty?"

He stared at me and spoke like he was drunk. "It's not dirty, nephew. Everyone here thinks it is a beautiful place, with fresh air; and they really want to live here."

"What? Fresh air... want to live here?"

"Ghost Environment" 59

"Well. The longer you are here, the better it gets. Of course, if you don't believe me, ask anyone."

I do not know how such a dirty place could be viewed as beautiful. Maybe this uncle is crazy. Because I still don't believe him, I'm going to ask some other people. I asked one person after another, but the answer was the same as the one I got from the big-belly uncle. I thought that perhaps the people living here had a lower education. That's why they could not differentiate between filth and beauty. Well, I'm educated with a B.A. degree. It's time for me to use my education to help society. I want to explain the value of the environment to the people here and teach them to clean it up to make their life more comfortable, without so much disease making them sick.

I started to gather everyone together, then I told them my intent: I want them to understand environmental issues. But no one liked my proposal. And they thought I was a crazy, silly person who just wanted to destroy their way of life. I really did not understand. I've tried to learn from primary school through college, and I've spent a lot of money gaining my knowledge. Why did no one here value that? Gosh! If I am really so foolish, maybe I am cheating others. I have good intentions; but not only don't they see my good intent, they've seriously beaten me up. Why did they do this to me? I've never met such unkind people.

I sat by myself feeling upset. When suddenly, I remembered the quote: "Words alone are inadequate. The theory must be closely linked to the implementation." Well, I'll just try to be a role model by myself. Ultimately, they will follow my example.

After deciding this, I tried new things. I picked up the trash and separated the waste into different categories, such as raw waste and recyclables. I tried to seem happy doing this work to show them that cleaning up the environment is not difficult but happy work.

But everything did not go as I expected. They walked up to me glaring. They captured me and tied both hands behind my back. They threw me into the garbage heap. My situation now is no different from a dog that has fallen into the sewer. They are standing around me like ants around a sugar pot. They yell at me shouting threats in my ears, "If you want to stay alive, don't destroy this place, because it is our lives." I tried moving and finally the ties broke.

.   .   .   .

My forehead is dripping with sweat and I'm panting. I get up to turn on the light and go to the mirror. I see that I'm perfectly clean with no garbage stains. I thought I had died in that ghost environment. But now I realize it was just a dream.

Translation by Teri Yamada and NHIM Soknea, July 2015

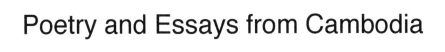

62   *Modern Literature of Cambodia*

CHIN Meas was born on September 3, 1980, in Teangpphleng village, Kampong Cham province. In 2007 he received a monk's certificate for teaching Buddhism and in 2010 he received a BA in Cambodian literature from Khemarah University in Phnom Penh. During this time he served as an ordained monk. He is a prolific poet and novella writer and is currently working on a collection of essays. Many of his poems have a Buddhist resonance with cautionary themes about greed and desire.

Piggybank

They take care, protect, and guard
each caring for the piggy bank,
putting coins in every day
even though the piggy bank doesn't care.

The piggy bank has a hopeful smile in expectation
now thinking that in the future
    he will be rich and famous,
he is full of money in his stomach
        so loved by his owners,
who are taking especially good care of him
        even better now than before,

But the owners' thinking is very different
        from the piggy bank's,
they break it and take the money,
and the piggy bank is destroyed,
dead because of the money.

Rahula* Swallows the Moon

Rahula is trying to catch the moon late at night,
swallowing it without pity,
without caring about the earth and the sky,
devouring all the light from the world.

He greedily swallows the whole moon himself,
he swallows the moon without fearing anyone,
thinking only of his own stomach,
swallowing it all out of violence and ignorance.

*Rahula: Indian mythology narrates the story of Rahula or Rahu. It is said that Vishnu cut off Rahula's head after he stole the elixir of immortality from the gods. In turn, angry at the sun and moon for revealing him to Vishnu, Rahu's immortal severed head pursues and temporarily swallows them, thus causing an eclipse.

Remote Control

Entertainment TV has many channels,
various kinds of programs and different stories,
each program follows a certain set time,
if you want to watch, press the remote control.

You can watch anything you desire,
you can change to any channel,
when you press, another channel, okay,
happy with the program, copy it to view again.

Now tired of watching it, wanting to change it again,
whether night or day,
the remote control is happy to be changed,
from an old story to a new story instantaneously.

64 *Modern Literature of Cambodia*

YENG Chheangly was born on October 9, 1988, in Kandal province. He received a BA in business and hospitality from the University of Human Resources in Phnom Penh. Currently he works in the customer service division at Mobitel. The poem "Strobe Lights" won the second place prize for poetry in the 2013 Nou Hach Literary Awards competition. Many of his poems have themes concerned with social justice and the environment.

Strobe Lights

Awesome! This nightclub in the city
its strobe lights brightly flashing,
light swirling everywhere
shimmering in all colors.

Bright light permeates
all corners illuminated,
tonight, happiness fills this club
fears and worries, dissipated.

Colorful light fills the inside
outside, pitch black darkness,
hungry lives walking, exploring
without the same clarifying light.

Translated by Teri Shaffer Yamada and NHIM Soknea, 2013

Recycle Bottle Collector

She drags the cart forward along the roadside
from dawn to dusk in her ragged clothes,
dirty, full of dust, and looking awful, she tirelessly
picks up every bottle to recycle along the way.

She reaches deeper and deeper into piles of trash
to improve her chances for discovering more bottles,
collecting every one, no matter how smelly or dirty
she cares about nothing but this.

Traveling from place to place in dirty, stinking clothes
followed by many flies chasing the smelly bottles in her cart,
she continues on, dragging the cart back home
reeking with garbage stench.

Undeterred, her little brother claps his hands in welcome
singing happily; hugging, kissing and touching her,
with the simple question
"Sister! Do you have any food?"

Rendition by YENG Chheangly and Teri Yamada, 2015

66 *Modern Literature of Cambodia*

SUY Vansak's poem "A Warrior's Spirit" won the first place prize for poetry in the 2008 Nou Hach Literary Awards competition. It reflects the plight of many disabled veterans who sacrificed so much for peace in Cambodia during the civil war.

A Warrior's Spirit

Reminiscing about the past,
As a soldier protecting Cambodians.
I was a powerful fighter,
Winning every battle.

Fighting the enemy,
Paving the way for Cambodians to avoid suffering.
Wishing Cambodians happiness,
Removing them from civil strife.

Now the war is coming to an end,
For everyone, everywhere.
Peace is shining brightly,
Certainly on Cambodian land.

I'm joyously happy,
As a soldier who loves his nation.
I love my motherland like anyone else,
Longing for peace in the country.

Even though I'm a cripple now,
A beggar in the markets and bus station.
I raise my hands in prayer to everyone,
Asking for survival and peace.

Translation in 2008 by the Nou Hach Literary Association
translation team

Venerable KREUN Yoeun's poem "Buffaloes" received the second place prize for poetry in the 2008 Nou Hach Literary Awards competition. This poem expresses the Buddhist cautionary theme about the karmic consequences of greed and excess.

Buffaloes

A man is plowing,
Plowing with buffaloes.
The land is cracked and dry,
Plowing under the torrid sun,
Blistering hot,
No kindness in plowing,
No pity on buffaloes.

Plowing is so endless,
Plowing improperly,
Plowing rows to wake the soil,
The vast field,
By tired buffaloes,
With nothing to eat,
No water, no grass.

Plowing in April,
Plowing without reason,
Not our ancestors' way,
Plowing fields without water,
Wishful thinking to get good crops,
For profit,
To become a millionaire.

Plowing is already done,
The ploughshare has been put away,
Removing the buffaloes from the yoke,

68   *Modern Literature of Cambodia*

Tying them under the mango tree,
Ignoring them,
Enjoying the crops,
The buffaloes suffer.

The buffaloes collapse,
Sleeping on the hill,
Straw covers their faces,
With sleepy eyes,
Eating rotten straw,
The buffaloes suffer,
Feeling pain in their whole body.

The master laughs happily,
But the buffaloes die,
Their meat sold at market,
The liver, stomach, and intestines are left,
For the master to eat while drinking wine,
The dogs get the bones,
The skin is peeled for hide.

Translation in 2008 by the Nou Hach Literary Association
translation team

Sophiline Cheam Shapiro was born in 1967 in Phnom Penh. She was eight-years-old when the Khmer Rouge evacuated her family from Phnom Penh. Later she became one of the first students to learn classical dance and graduated from the re-established School of Fine Arts in Phnom Penh. Along with her husband, she founded the Khmer Arts Academy in Long Beach, California to teach a new generation of Cambodian-Americans the traditional art and culture of Cambodia. She is an innovative choreography who collaborates with composers and designers to creative new dance forms that maintain the integrity of classical Khmer dance. The autobiographical essay below is based on a talk given at the 2014 Nou Hach Literary Association Conference in Phnom Penh.

Dancing Stories

I have recently begun work on a new dance project with the working title of *The Kings of Desire*. It may seem strange (or even an invitation for bad luck) to write about a project that I have yet to finish, but it helps to illustrate how storytelling has changed during my 33-year career as a Khmer classical dancer.

I was born before the onset of civil war, but I began my dance training as a member of the first generation to study and perform classical dance after the defeat of the Khmer Rouge regime. At that time, our teachers were desperate to revive the dance as they had known it in the royal palace prior to the fall of Phnom Penh. My fellow dance students and I worked hard to rebuild a tradition of pedagogy and performance. Within a few years, we were touring our country and the parts of the world that would recognize our existence (at that time, mostly the Soviet Union and India), helping to remind everyone we could that Cambodia was heir to more magnificent traditions than auto-genocide.

Khmer classical dance has always told stories. And we

70   *Modern Literature of Cambodia*

students were dancing mythology and folklore that had been handed down from generation to generation. Nevertheless, classical dance was never a static form. The dance emerged as a form of ritual prayer among the sandstone temples of Angkor and then became a form of court entertainment within the royal palace. In the 1960s, with the construction of proscenium stages (The Preah Saramarith Theater, Chaktomuk Hall), the dancers of the court created shorter, non-narrative dances that celebrated the country's new sense of post-colonial nationalism. Even during the 1980s, students and faculty at the School of Fine Arts choreographed dances that celebrated contemporary treaties and the enduring friendship of aligned nations. But by the end of that decade, our main focus remained on revival.

In 1990, Cambodia received invitations to send troupes of classical dancers to the Edinburgh Festival in Scotland and the Los Angeles Festival in the USA. These were significant because they represented our first opportunity to show the Western world—which refused to acknowledge us politically— that our venerable culture remained intact. I was a member of the second troupe. At the LA Festival and on a subsequent national tour, we performed iconic dances of our teachers' generation (*Chun Por, Apsara, Tep Monorom*) and story ballets that were much older (*Reamker, Ream Eyso* and *Moni Mekhala*). We did not perform any of the highly politicized dances created during our own era. In fact, we were performing virtually the same program as that of the last tour of Khmer dancers to the USA, which had taken place in 1971. Cambodian refugees in the USA embraced us out of a sense of nostalgia for a happier moment in history while some vilified us for our association with a contemporary regime they had fled.

Within a year, I had married an American citizen and immigrated to Los Angeles. Not long after, the Paris Peace Accords were adopted and the West once again established diplomatic relations with Cambodia. In the U.S., I began teaching the classical canon to Khmer American children and performing traditional dances at festivals. In Cambodia, the recently returned royalty began celebrating the dance as it had been performed before the 1970 coup d'état that overthrew then Prince Sihanouk. American foundations, including the Rockefeller Foundation and the Asian Cultural Council, began funding revival projects. As a result, the 1990s became a decade that looked backwards with an emphasis on repeating stories of the past rather than on examining the present. It is telling that in 2001, the program for the next tour of dancers from the School of Fine Arts to the USA was almost identical to the tours of 1971 and 1990. Though I continue to love and admire these beautiful dances, I could understand if an outside observer looked at these three tours and concluded that the Cambodian imagination had gone into hibernation 30 years earlier.

In 1998, while a graduate student at UCLA, one of my professors left an application for a choreographic grant in my mailbox. Intrigued, I considered what I might propose to do if I was lucky enough to receive funding. After all, I had not choreographed a single dance since my graduation from middle school. But during the previous few years I had become fascinated by Shakespeare's play *Othello*, which I had read in a college class titled: English as Critical Thinking. In *Othello*, I found many parallels between Shakespeare's heroine Desdemona and Neang Seda, the heroine of the *Reamker*. I also saw reflections of my own experiences marrying a foreign husband and living abroad. So I decided to turn *Othello* into a Khmer classical dance. At the time, I had no idea what a radical proposition this was. It was just something I wanted to do.

I received the Irvine Fellowship in Dance and returned to Cambodia in 1999 to set my dance drama on my former colleagues at the School of Fine Arts (which had changed its name to the Royal University of Fine Arts or RUFA). For eight years I had been living in the USA, where self-initiated arts projects are the norm. So, I arrived in Cambodia with money, ideas and initiative of my own, and set about making a dance,

72 *Modern Literature of Cambodia*

Samritechak, that, because it was intriguing to me, I assumed would resonate with my fellow artists and audiences. Fortunately for me it did. We premiered it at a packed RUFA Theater in 2000 and toured it subsequently to Hong Kong, the USA and Italy.

Until that moment, Khmer classical dance had been for the most part an instrument of the powerful, whether the temple, the palace, the government or the military. It was a top-down art form that served to reinforce the authority of its patrons. But in 1999, I, an individual artist, made a successful dance that, while remaining true to the form's aesthetic conventions, came into being for no other reason than the fact that I was inspired to interpret my contemporary world. *Samritechak* established two important precedents: it reminded the field that classical dance could once again be contemporary and, for the first time, that it could be used as an instrument for personal interpretation and expression.

Over the next decade, I choreographed dances that explored the ambiguous relationship between women and traditional culture, the transformation of identity among immigrants, and the dangers of extreme rhetoric and cycles of violence. Aside from two experimental, non-narrative dances, all of my dances told stories that interpreted modern history as I had experienced it.

During the same time, other members of my generation began experimenting within their own fields, most notably Rithy Panh in cinema, Him Sophy in music and Sopheap Pich in the visual arts. So I began to think about how some of us might work together to tell stories for our time and came up with a new project, *A Bend in the River.* In *Bend,* we took a traditional folktale, combined elements from other stories, and rewrote it so that it became a contemplation on the urge for and repulsion from the notion of revenge among a generation that had suffered so much loss. For this project, Sopheap Pich created rattan crocodile puppets and Him Sophy wrote the first new music for pin peat ensemble in modern history. I couldn't have been happier with the result. Besides the beau-

"Dancing Stories" 73

ty of the dance itself, I felt that we were establishing a path for collaborative storytelling among Cambodian artists—something I'd never seen before. In the twenty-first century, we need not wait for some authority to assign us work nor do we need to work in isolation. Instead, we can generate our own ideas and work together to realize them.

This brings me back to *The Kings of Desire*, another project on which I'm collaborating with Him Sophy. When complete, it is intended to be the first classical dance that takes place amid a history in which I have lived. It is a fictionalized retelling of that dramatic 1990 tour of Cambodian dancers to the USA. It will portray no gods; it will contain no magical creatures. Instead, it will explore the dynamics at play as Cambodia began to interact with a wider world as it emerged from extraordinary isolation, war and poverty. If successful, it will further establish the power of classical dance to tell stories that interpret contemporary society.

Poetry and Essays
by Cambodian Americans

YIN Luoth, an essayist, poet and fiction writer, was born on November 17,1951 in Samrong Chongkal, Siem Reap, Oddar Mean Chey. He completed a BA in Political Science at Seattle University, Washington, in the United States and earlier a Diploma in Literature in Phnom Penh, Cambodia. He frequently travels back to Cambodia.

As a Poet: An Essay

My sad life leads me to see other's sadness including humans, animals and other creatures, and the only way I can find to express this sympathetic feeling is through writing poetry.

My mother taught me to be a poet. She was sad and full of sorrow after my father passed away when I was young. She had to console herself and our three siblings the most she could in a small village far away from the city. I remember when I was about 10 years old, she recited an old poem to me from the "The Fable of December" once at dawn at the end of rainy season; it ran:

Wistful for December,
The wind blows, the water recedes,
The distant, soft sound of thunder in the south,
Thunder claps responding to one another,
At the end of each rainy season, the thunder must depart.

Thunders' advice:
"All the trees grow deeper roots,
All crabs and snails dig deeper holes;
After we depart, take care."

This poem caused me to be sympathetic with nature. My young mind had an active imagination believing that the

76   *Modern Literature of Cambodia*

thunder could speak to crabs, snails and trees, and that those creatures could understand it. I started to like poetry when I was little and spent most of my time reading any book I encountered. There were not many books in our village, so my mother had to borrow monthly national magazines from a secretary of the district office, who lived close by.

My mother's dream was implanted in my mind early on. She told me that when she was pregnant with me, she dreamed that an official person—an assistant to the chief of the district, in my village—gave her a mirror, untarnished with a good frame. She interpreted the dream to mean that she would have a son who would be bright like a mirror. My mother's interpretation has lingered in my doubtful mind, wondering if I can justify myself as a brilliant person since I was a poor student in junior high school, especially in science. The only subject I did well in was literature.

My literary works justified my mother's dream. I have published three books of poetry and three novellas. Three of my books were translated in English. My poems have been published many times in the United States, by local newspapers, journals, and the National Library of Poetry, which awarded me the Editor's Choice Award. Lately, one of my poems was selected by John Gallas and published in *The Song Atlas: A Book of World Poetry* (2002) in England, from among poems and poets of 196 countries. One of my poems represents Cambodian Poetry Princeton University's *Encyclopedia of Poetry.* In Cambodia, my books have been widely read. One university has used them for in-class discussion. The Royal Academy of Letters recommended my poems to their students. My poems and essays have been published in a prominent newspaper in Cambodia. I was invited by radio and TV stations for interviews about my books. So far, my literary works have given me recognition as a Cambodian poet—an established poet since these works have been gradually appreciated by both Cambodian and

Western audiences. With some of these credentials, I feel that my readers can use my poems as a mirror that reflects social reality in Cambodia.

My intent now is to improve the quality of my writing. I believe the words of Vincent Van Gogh: "Where there is sympathy, life is restored." I have tried to apply this idea to my writing in order to invoke awareness and sympathy in my readers, in anticipation that my writing may help to restore unfortunate lives.

Yin Luoth represents a modernist trend in Cambodian poetry. The poems below were written in 2013 with socially critical themes reflecting trends in modern Cambodian society.

Poor Boy in a Modern Time

Ipad, Ipod so exciting,
I know you are poor, mom,
But I make myself beg you
For any chance of help.
Being born in this modern time,
So many people
Making immeasurable progress.
It's upsetting without a phone
When all my friends have one.

Modern Rice Field

The rice field in old times
Husband with wife harvest.
Now it's the cool season,
The wife harvests alone
Mother with child in a hammock.
Where is the husband?
Has he gone to the city
To look for dollars?

Mekong River

I used to flow
Easily,
Living peacefully with Khmer,
Providing fertilizer
And all kinds of fish.
But now I suffer,
They take my sand
And expand my small islands,
Narrow my way.
What would I say?
I have no choice.
During the rainy season,
I flood and people suffer.
I don't know if they understand?

Oh greed!
Oh ignorance!

"The poet's gift and artistic responsibility is to express the sorrow and beauty of life for those who cannot." Charles Schultz

Lexus

I am Lexus
The ultimate car,
Anyone riding me
Is magnificent.

Wherever they go
Winning popularity,
Through wealth and money
Whether a big or small shot.

On the land
Both men and women depend on me,
A new car
To sustain their honor.

My Neighbors

I am feeling sorry for my neighbors
Outside the city.
They think I'm a rich man
Come from the U.S.
They believe I'm a nice person
Because I'm not acting out
Like a local big shot.
They come to borrow money,
When I tell them I don't have it
They don't believe me.
Believing in the U.S.,
There is a money tree.
I feel sorry for my neighbors.

80 *Modern Literature of Cambodia*

Bunkong TUON was born in Cambodia several years before the 1975 communist takeover of the country and lived under the Khmer Rouge regime without understanding what was happening around him. His mother passed away from sickness and starvation. In 1979, his uncles, aunts, and grandmother took him with them as they fled to refugee camps along the Cambodia-Thailand border, while his father stayed behind with his new wife. With the help of an American sponsor, he and his family arrived in Malden, Massachusetts, in 1981. Currently he teaches ethnic literature at Union College, in Schenectady, New York. BK Tuon's creative work has appeared in The Massachusetts Review, The Truth About the Fact: International Journal of Literary Nonfiction, NYADP Journal, genre, and Khmer Voice in Poetry. NQY Books published his first collection of poetry, Gruel, in 2015. The essay below was first published in Numéro Cinq Magazine, IV.2 (2013) and is reprinted with permission of the publisher.

On Fathers, Losses, and Other Influences: Essay — Bunkong Tuon

This is a poignant, moving essay about loss, fathers, books, and writing. It is a lament and a confession. It is also a strangely hopeful message for us all.

Maybe it was the wine in me that made me blurt out, "You know, I'm annoyed with having to defend us all the time. The writers I read in my twenties saved my life!" Then I began to tell the story of how I fumbled into a local library, picked up a book from the shelf, read it from cover to cover, then went back to the same aisle and chose other books by that same author. I told my friends how the author spoke to me that day and how he changed my life.

"On Fathers, Losses and Other Influences" 81

This happened at a party to celebrate the end of another academic term. We were talking about the plight of the Humanities. A few years ago, a local university eliminated several language, literature, and culture departments. That fall, the President told the American people that, in order to build a strong future for our nation, we must support our education system—only math and science were specifically mentioned as important areas for development. In the face of the current 7.9 percent unemployment rate, all of us knew how hard it was to talk about the values of the Humanities to our students, to explain to them why reading, discussing, and writing about literary texts matter.

The hostess of the party, a good friend, asked, "So tell us, BK. Who was that author you were reading?"

And I couldn't utter his name. I was ashamed of him.

Once in an interview with the Franco-Swiss director Barbet Schroeder, this writer got mad drunk, cursed his wife, and literally kicked her off the sofa. He was not a good man, but he was my literary father.

As for my biological father, I have written about him with pride. My poems are a kind of love letter from an orphan to a father he never knew. In "Cambodia: Memory and Desire," I wrote, "My father sold ice cream in train stations,/ competing with street peddlers with his/ good looks and easy talk" (323). In "Lies I told about Father," I went even further with my admiration.

> With a son's quiet adoration, I chiseled you:
> a gangster from the East, a Khmer Krom
> whose veins bled out Khmer characters (not Vietnamese),
> who, guided by fate, found himself in the West
> and married mother for her virtue and beauty.

82   *Modern Literature of Cambodia*

> In my poems you drink because, well, real men
> drink, curse, and sleep around (the cursing
> and sleeping around, you didn't do, of course,
> because of your love and respect for Mother).

My father is mythic in my writing. He is clearly someone I'm not: a "gangster" with a sense of adventure, a man's man who can hold his liquor and charm his way out of troubles with "good looks and easy talk." The truth is: I never knew my father. He passed away in Cambodia in the 1980s, while I was a high school student in Malden, MA. When my grandmother, uncles, and aunts left for the UN camps along the Thailand-Cambodia border in 1979, my father decided to stay in Cambodia with his new family. Like many other Cambodians who had fallen victim to Pol Pot, his wife, my mother, had passed away from sickness and starvation under the Khmer Rouge regime in 1976 or so. My father took another wife several years later, when Vietnamese forces liberated Cambodia. Fearful that, as a stepson, I might be mistreated by my new family, my grandmother took me away from my father, carrying me on her back as she and her children trekked across the border, avoiding landmines and jungle pirates, to where the UN had set up a camp, rumored to have an abundance of food and medicine.

This is the story I've inherited from my grandmother, aunts, and uncles. It is the story of a father I never knew, and, in the absence of knowledge, I have the freedom to invent him in any way I want. Out of a desire to be like my cousins who have the good fortune to have fathers, I "chiseled" him, in that freedom that only imagination provides and that desires shape, in a way that made sense to me, an orphan refugee child. In my writing about him, I never once mentioned the stepmother and my half-brothers. The father possesses masculine qualities, or what, at the time, I imagined "masculinity" to be, with the hope that someday I would inherit

"On Fathers, Losses and Other Influences"   83

those qualities myself: rough on the outside but gentle on the inside, good looking and, more importantly, good with words. He is not necessarily a man of letters. As long as he is comfortable in a social setting, able to leap with ease from one social group to the next, then this man is my father. He is the father I never knew; he is the father I created.

The literary father, the one I knew, is the one I'm embarrassed about. He is Charles Bukowski, the Los Angeles poet of the damned. In his own belligerent way, the guy saved me, saved me from an early death of the mind and spirit. In the early 90s, I was working for a maintenance service company in Long Beach, California. From six in the evening to four in the morning, I'd go to people's houses, offices, private and religious schools and scrub their tubs, mop their floors, and empty their trash. Before that, I'd worked at my aunt's donut shop in Bell, California. I was never good at customer service. Although I didn't get fired, my aunt was quietly relieved when I found a job elsewhere. And before being a failed donut maker in Southern California, I was a college dropout in eastern Massachusetts. One day, I just stopped attending classes at Bunker Hill Community College. I had gone there because a friend's mother had taken me by the hand, had driven me to the campus, and had enrolled me. And before community college, I had been a high school punk who had ditched classes one day to go skateboarding, had forged my grandmother's signature the following day, had been busted and had been sent back home for a two-day suspension. The school graduated me because they didn't want me to come back. They didn't know what to do with me, just as I didn't know what I was doing reading Shakespeare and Chaucer in English classes. Neither the books nor the teachers could explain why I felt so different from my surroundings. Nothing made sense.

But, for some reason, the world according to Bukowski did make sense to me. On that day in the local branch of the Long

84   *Modern Literature of Cambodia*

Beach Public Library, Bukowski spoke to me. I can still remember that day: a typical sunny Southern California day, nothing strange about it. I got up about ten in the morning after a night of cleaning toilets, mopping floors, and emptying trash bins, and mysteriously, I felt an urge, a summoning, to go to the library. I borrowed my uncle's car, drove to the nearest library, and sat in its parking lot, watching children and their parents going in and out and thinking about that closeness—that intimacy and trust with another human which seemed to evade me somehow. Once the parking lot was empty of people, I got out of the car and made a beeline for the library's entrance, which I walked quickly through, eyes downcast, towards the walls of books on one side of the large room, where I could hide myself. I roamed in aisles of books until I found myself in front of the A-B row, picking up and putting back several books until I came to *Play the Piano Drunk like a Percussion Instrument until the Fingers Begin to Bleed a Bit.* The world then opened up for me.

It was a world of men and women who had lost their way, a world of sadness and cruelty with occasional beauty, a world of outsiders living on the cultural margins. Somehow the filth he described in those poems felt pure and honest, and the madness seemed sane, a logical outcome of being exiled from Eden for so long. Writing, for me, and I think for Bukowski too, has to do with working with that state of exile, where loss is the center of many ghostly things and homelessness is what you have always known. I don't think we can ever fill that void, so we write about it. No matter how much we believe in the transformative power of words and the imagination, loss is eternal.

After devouring *Play the Piano Drunk*, I began picking out other poetry books by Bukowski and reading them in that section of the A-B row: *Burning in Water, Drowning in Flame, The Days Run Away like Wild Horses over the Hills, Dangling in the Tournefortia*, and that wonderful collection of poems and

"On Fathers, Losses and Other Influences"   85

short stories, *Septuagenarian Stew*. I can't imagine what it would be like to sleep in roach-infested bungalows and seedy motel rooms, buy cheap wine by the gallon at a liquor store on L.A.'s skid row, or bet on luck at your local racetrack, but I could relate to the feelings of alienation, loss, desperation, and loneliness from which Bukowski's bums, drunks, gamblers, and prostitutes suffer. It was the feeling of being broken and living with it, although I knew then, just as I know now, that our brokenness has different sources. For me, it was that historical rupture of being ripped away from home—from my mother, my father, my Cambodia. My poetry collection, *Under the Tamarind Tree*, came out of this historical moment; it's a story of a refugee child trying to piece together the broken pieces of memory, of places and lost time, and rebuilding himself.

The title poem, for instance, has to do with my most powerful and early memory of loss, the death of my mother under the Khmer Rouge regime. Here is my exile from Eden.

> The child is sitting on the lap
> of his aunt, under the old tamarind tree
> outside the family home.
>
> The tree stands still, quiet
> and indifferent. The house sways
> on stilts cut from the bamboo tree
>
> in the backyard, where grandfather's garden lies.
> Monks in saffron robe, and nuns with shaved heads,
> their lips darkened with betel-nut stain, sit
>
> in the veranda of the family home, chanting prayers
> for the child's mother in *Pali*, which sounds like
> a nursery song from which the boy is excluded.
>
> Incense perfumes the hot dry air.

86   *Modern Literature of Cambodia*

There emerges a strange familiar song
between the child and his aunt that day—
a distant song, melodic but somehow harsh,
as if the strings are drawn too tight—

Each time the child hears Buddhist prayers
coming from the house, he cries;
each time he cries, the aunt, a girl herself,
pinches the boy's thigh.

The boy cries because he doesn't understand
why strangers are making noise while his mother
is trying to sleep. His aunt pinches the child's thigh
because it is her first taste of loss.

The Khmer Rouge eliminated from their utopia, their Cambodia in Year Zero, any trace of Western influences, which they saw as corroding the country's moral and cultural fiber. Schools, banks, the free market, hospitals, and religion were abolished. Monks were forced to defrock or face death. That was how my grandmother came to marry her second husband, the only grandfather I knew. But, in this poem, I gave my mother a proper funeral rite. In the face of filial duty and an orphan's desire to do something right for a mother he never knew, I gave her the dignity and respect of which the Khmer Rouge had deprived her and many others.

On that day in the library, I also found in Bukowski a voice that was clear, direct, and raw. I was a kid who had barely made it through high school only to become a community college dropout, but I actually understood what I was reading. There were no tricks, gimmicks, and secret codes to be deciphered by the select few, the educated and well-informed readers. When the wellspring of Bukowski's poetry books ran dry at that library (the Dana Branch of the Long Beach Public Library), I turned to his semi-autobiographical novels. *Post Office*, the book that put Bukowski on the map, wasn't exactly

"On Fathers, Losses and Other Influences" **87**

Ulysses or *Finnegans Wake,* and *Ham on Rye* was no *A Portrait of the Artist as a Young Man.* But they were easy for me, a college dropout, to understand. Bukowski was a writer for the common man, who recognizes immediately when someone is in pain, when he is burning in water and drowning in flame. Pain is pain: it's immediate and real, and Bukowski was good at capturing it unflinchingly.

So free, so private, so enormous, that moment in the library, that rebirth, and like any birth, so full of possibilities, so hopeful, so alive. In "How Everything Changed," I described what happened to me that day:

> It was in one such corner, hidden away
> from the sight and sound of suburban
> mothers and their children, where I
> picked a random book off the shelf:
> a book of poems by that drunken
> old man, a book filled with social misfits
> and outcasts, drunks and prostitutes,
> barflies, cockroaches, and vomit;
> at that moment, I felt my first breath.
> I was gasping for air.
> I felt my own sweet suffering in others.
> Loneliness was extinguished,
> and compassion bloomed in my chest.
> I am telling you this, so that you know
> in the worst storm of your life this mad love
> can hit you, smashing you into a billion pieces,
> interconnecting with everyone and everything.

On that day, I was somebody new. I didn't want to die anymore. After the poems, short stories, and novels (it had to be in that order, for my child's mind was still learning to build a mental picture from each joining of words) came the essays, where Bukowski introduced me, in his own arrogant way, to other writers. Somewhere, somehow, in that web of intertext-

88　　*Modern Literature of Cambodia*

ual electricity, I came to Hemingway and Carver, the French poets (Rimbaud, Baudelaire, and Genet, who scribbled his own dirty notes in prison), and the Russians like Chekhov, Tolstoy, and that great psychologist and spiritual advisor, Fyodor Dostoyevsky.

I wanted to be a writer then, but I knew I couldn't write. I didn't have an education. I enrolled myself at Long Beach City College, taking classes that interested me, classes in philosophy, history, anthropology, and English—relearning the basic skills of reading and writing and returning to those books I was required to read in high school and couldn't get through the first page. I remember reading late into the night Shakespeare's *King Lear* for an English class and being moved to tears. (Many years later, as an English professor, I watched a Shakespeare & Company's performance of the play with friends from the college, and I still couldn't hold back the tears.) As for Chaucer, I found his *Canterbury Tales* as dirty as, heck, even raunchier than Bukowski's *Notes of a Dirty Old Man.*

I also remember walking into a local pawn shop and buying a used typewriter, the one where the keys got stuck after striking the second or third letter. Still, I typed the night away on that thing, while my aunt slept in her room and my uncle made donuts at his shop in Bell. I remember the cockroaches coming out of their crevices to keep me company. It was magical then; the tuition was cheap, something like 200 bucks for each semester, and I had few responsibilities other than to read and write whatever I wanted. I wrote songs and poems, with occasional flash fiction thrown into the mix. The writing was amateurish at best; the topics were the usual explorations of angst, love, and death, but there were a handful of poems that were honest, reflecting my life experience, such as "Early Saturday Morning in Malden, MA (1986)":

> Saturday morning
> grocery shopping at the only Asian
> market in the city;
> putting back fish sauce and soy sauce,
> picking up milk, bread, and cereal,
> I told Grandma to be quiet—
>
> Because Jeanine and her mother were there too.

When I had too many credits at LBCC, they gave me an Associate Degree and transferred me to California State University in Long Beach, where I took a poetry workshop with Gerald Locklin. Locklin was a rock star to me. He was the only person I met who had met the man himself, drank with him, and invited him to read at the university. Bukowski had already been dead several years; so Locklin was as close as I could ever get to my literary father.

After Long Beach, I went to graduate school at the University of Massachusetts in Amherst. I was simply fearful of the life of poverty that Knut Hamsun's nameless character had suffered in *Hunger*. I knew enough of hunger in the refugee camps to keep me from falling into romantic revelries about the starving artist. In graduate school, I did what I had to do. Most of my time was spent deciphering the works of Derrida, Foucault, Lacan, Bhabha, and other theorists. Nevertheless, I managed to eke out a memoir, *Under the Tamarind Tree,* on which my poetry collection is based.

Then I won the academic version of winning the lottery: I got a job after graduation.

I now teach at a private liberal arts college in upstate New York, working with students whose life stories aren't exactly like mine. I've shared my story with those students who have come to my office and seem to have lost their way, reminding them of the magic and possibilities in life's offerings, of finding

90   *Modern Literature of Cambodia*

one's voice and passion and, in the words of Joseph Campbell, of following one's own bliss. But I have yet to talk openly with my colleagues about Bukowski without feeling anxious. At a place where I can't afford the cars that some of my students drive, I feel embarrassed, inadequate, that the writer who influenced me, who gave me life, was a bum who roamed skid row, jumping from one rooming house to the next, working odd jobs and writing in roach-infested motel rooms, cursing the world for worshiping other writers while forsaking him, being god-awful mean to women and men, to whites and blacks alike. I already feel different enough with the way I look and how much money I have in my bank account; I don't want to also feel different intellectually.

Listen, I'm not suffering from what Harold Bloom calls the anxiety of influence. I don't have an oedipal complex with Bukowski: I'm neither denying his influence nor trying to topple him, nor do I tremble under the shadow of his great name or from holding his books in my hands. I know who I am, know where I came from, and know what kind of stories I like to tell. Maybe, as is the case with our biological fathers, we don't choose our literary fathers, no matter who they happen to be. Maybe Carver is right. "Influences are forces— circumstances, personalities, irresistible as the tide," he writes in "Fires." Carver became a poet and a master of the short story because he didn't have time to work on a novel. When he was learning his craft, Carver was a young father who had little money and felt overwhelmed by parental responsibilities. He tells us:

> During those ferocious years of parenting, I usually didn't have the time, or the heart, to think about working on anything very lengthy. The circumstances of my life, the 'grip and slog' of it, in D. H. Lawrence's phrase, did not permit it. The circumstances of my life with these children dictated something else. They said if I wanted to write any-thing, and finish it, and if ever I wanted to take satisfaction

out of finished work, I was going to have to stick to stories and poems. (34)

Under "those ferocious years," Carver didn't have a room of his own in which to develop his craft. It was his teacher, John Gardner, who offered the young writer his office in Chico State University to write on weekends. So, by necessity, by circumstance, Carver became Carver.

As for me, I became who I am because of Bukowski, because of the circumstances surrounding my early years, because I left home and lost my way.

I wish I could go back to that party and, without hesitation, without much anxiety, answer my friend's questions, "Who was the writer who influenced you so much? What was the book that you read in that library?"

He was Charles Bukowski, a poet from L.A. The book was *Play the Piano Drunk like a Percussion Instrument until the Fingers Begin to Bleed a Bit*.

––

Works Cited

- Carver, Raymond. *Fires: Essays, Poems, Stories*. New York: Vintage Books, 1989.
- Tuon, Bunkong. "Cambodia: Memory and Desire." *The Massachusetts Review*. 45.3 (2004): 319-329.

Inheritance

(republished from *Gruel* with permission of the author)

My uncles, aunts, and grandmother all agree:
It was a difficult time. People starving.
You don't trust the children. You don't trust
your neighbors, friends, even your family.
But this can't be. It must be something I read.
Something I taught, pointed out in a lecture,
maybe discovered in a conversation with a survivor,
a man with ashen hair and toothless smile,
in an apartment complex in Lowell, MA.

Anyway, these are the images I carry with me:
rib cage thin. Diarrhea. Chicken blindness. Dysentery.
Hands tied behind your back, legs too weak to crawl, eyes
bulging,
white with petrifaction, irises black as night, wings broken,
spirit destroyed, only paranoia and hunger ruled the day
and the night, my mother's body, difficulty with breathing,
bones sharp as knives, eternal loneliness, eternal sadness,
the sour taste of tamarind, Mother dead from starvation,
her sister, a branch in hand, sharpened by hunger,
hunting for lizards, snakes, crickets, for dark green leaves,
all black—black pajamas, black hair, black sadness,
always night, always cold, cold wind and loneliness,
fear of whispering wind and unseen eyes, pineapple eyes,
everywhere and nowhere, strangers, friends, family
disappearing, without struggle, without a sound,
the only evidence is the fear in those trembling,
working the fields, lips so dry it hurts when it rains,
the corpses strewn about as if for a group pose,
in a ditch along the dirt road, plastic bag wrapped
around the heads, a statement on the value
of human life, unworthy of a single bullet.

"Inheritance" 93

Their motto: to kill you is no loss, but what is
lost is family, the old way of life, being human,
and what is gained is a new world order,
monks disrobed, temples destroyed, elders useless,
the new temple is a pyramid of human skulls,
where a boy, illiterate and verging on puberty,
dressed in black pajamas, an AK-47 on his back,
a *kromar* around his neck, guards the entrance,
his old family gone, his new family is the organization,
his new mother is hate, his new father is Angka,
to which everything must be reported, Angka,
the figurehead, the godhead, the master of the universe,
from which, to which, everything revolves, the giver
and taker of life, human or otherwise, the maker of reality.

The Day My Worst Fear Came True
(republished from *Gruel* with permission of the author)

The restaurant was unremarkable,
hidden between a coffee shop and a Vietnamese
noodle place, within walking distance of
Portland State University. Our waitress
came over, filled our empty glasses,
a small Siam elephant tattooed on her right wrist,
and introduced herself as "Jennifer"
before leaving us to our menus.
Seeing a dish of papaya salad on a table
next to ours, I whispered to my wife,
"It's been a long time since I had Thai food."
When Jennifer returned,
I asked for beef in *Mussaman* curry
and chicken *Pad Ga Prau.*
I knew I couldn't finish both dishes, but I was greedy.
With a smile, I told the waitress to make it hot, extra spicy,
pointing to the four chilies icon on the menu.

94 *Modern Literature of Cambodia*

"Are you sure?" She looked concerned.
"It's very spicy. Have you guys been here before?"
We shook our heads.
"We usually recommend to our new customers medium hot:
two chilies max."
Having been to Thai restaurants on the East Coast,
I smiled, "I'm Asian. I grew up eating this type of food.
I think I can handle it."

Jennifer went to the kitchen to place our order.
I thought the matter was settled, when minutes later,
Jennifer and a gentleman in khaki pants and blue shirt
emerged from the kitchen. "Sir, the 'four chilies' is very spicy.
Are you sure you want it that hot? We usually recommend
our guests to try the medium hot first."
Slightly offended, I smiled: "Fine. Let's compromise. Give me
the three chilies, please. Thank you.
Waiting for my food, I thought to myself.
Maybe this will be it—the food that will transport me back
home,
to grandfather praising grandmother
for her fine cooking, an unusual gesture in our family.
When the food came, I was not disappointed.
The aroma of beef cooked tenderly in peanut sauce,
with potatoes, onion, carrots, and bell peppers,
reminded me of the beef curry at my family's home
during New Year and Ancestors Day.
The minced chicken with basils, chilies, and
lemongrass made the meat both sweet and spicy.
Heck, even my wife's vegetarian pad Thai dish was delicious!
I took a bite of the beef in *Mussaman* curry,
and tears began filling my eyes.
Soon enough, my nose was running, and my hair,
drenched with sweat, stuck to my forehead.
Concerned, Jennifer came over to our table and refilled
my water glass. I avoided her eyes.
As I continued to eat, nose dripping

"The Day My Worst Fear Came True"   95

and eyes watery, my wife didn't know
whether she should help me or ridicule me.
With ears ringing, I looked up and saw, once again,
Jennifer refilling my water glass.
My wife suggested that maybe
we should take the leftovers back to the hotel.
As firmly as I could, I said "No,"
and asked, "Isn't it enough that I suffer
such humiliation within the confines
of this restaurant? I don't want
to be walking on the streets of Portland
and announcing to the Pacific world
that I have lost my Khmer tongue."
I blew my nose into the napkin,
and she burst out laughing.

Prach LY, born in 1979 near Siem Reap and Battambang, fled with his family across fields of landmines to Thailand where they stayed for a year and a half. His family then relocated to the Philippines and finally Florida and later California. He grew up in Long Beach, California, and became the first influential Cambodian American hip-hop artist and rapper, appearing on Frontline and other media shows representing Cambodian American youth and their families' refugee experience. Many of his poems focus on the Cambodian genocide and its repercussions on Cambodian families.

art of faCt
PraCh

beyond the killing field,
a quarter of a century after the genocide.
after 2 million people murdered,
the other 5 million survive.
the fabric of the culture,
beauty drips the texture.
i find myself in Long Beach,
the next Cambodian mecca.
beside *srok Khmer, veal srae,* Angkor Wat,
some people still struggling,
on the aftermath of Pol Pot.

for some futures so bright, looks like high beams,
for others are lost in the American Dream.
for me it seems i'm on the road to no-where fast.
hitting speed bumps, drive'n in circles,
vehicle running out of gas.

there's a gap in our generation,
between the adults and kids.

"art of faCt" 97

but since i'm bilingual,
i'ma use communication as a bridge.
first i'ma knock down the walls,
between me and my parents,
listen to their stories an' all
without interference.
what they experience,
was evil at its darkest form.
their mind, body and heart,
shattered and torn.

the trauma of the war,
affect the refugee and foreigner.
suffering from deep depression,
post-traumatic stress disorder.
it's a new world order,
new threats that we're facing.
terrorist and INS deportation.
you can try to fight it go ahead be my guest,
cuz it's one strike and you're out of the U.S.

there's an epidemic that's killing us surely,
over things we don't even own,
like blocks and territories.
so call "OG" recruiting young ones.
jumping them in gangs,
giving them used guns.
not even old enuff to speak,
already hold'n heat,
walk'n a dangerous route,
talk'n about "code of the streets."

seek and you'll find,
the truth is where me hearts at.
i'm speak'n my mind,
and let my rhyme design this "art of faCt,"
line to line from front to back,

98 *Modern Literature of Cambodia*

from the heart of praCh,
comes the "art of faCt."

i've been asleep snore'n,
now i've awaken from my nap.
my brain been storming,
so i put on my think'n cap.
digging deeper into my mind,
at times i find it hard to hack.
but i'm a messenger this time,
delivering you this "art of faCt."

fast track, racers love cars,
spending every dollar and cents.
getting it all fix up, mix up in bad investments.
but that's their choice to choose,
some parents are still confuse,
the difference between,
discipline and child abuse.
i use to get whip and hit,
with wire and *ta-bong*.
it use to be a family matter,
until the law got involved.
for boys hang'n out,
that's ok, unlimited minutes.
for girls; what you talk'n about,
that's prohibited.
some is scared of it,
pushing them to the edge.
some parents still believe in,
fixing up marriage.

i inherited all of this,
the knowledge of the faCts.
being a Khmer that i am,
i feel the weight on my back.
but look what we're building,

"art of faCt" 99

right here in Long Beach.
a Cambodian Town,
down Anaheim streets.
the seed has been planted,
the foundation has been laid,
all it takes is time,
and *voilà* its all great!

i was raised not to be racist,
so my judgment is color blind fold.
to judge one by their action,
and keep that mind frame on hold!
we're gonna stick together,
like cook rice in a bowl.
open stores, markets,
products, merchandise...sold!
Business Bureau and Agencies,
to Chamber of Commerce.
fields in teaching, medical to law,
y'all we even running for offices.

there's hope in the kids,
their learning faster then we did,
traditional dances to classical music.
old method is still used,
you get sick, you get coined.
New Year's Celebration,
everybody in the world come and join.
i am proud to say;
" i'm a Khmer " with pride.
because i praCh,
refuse to let my culture die!

seek and you'll find,
the truth is where my heart's at.
i'm speak'n my mind
and let my rhyme design this "art of faCt."

100   *Modern Literature of Cambodia*

line to line, from front to back.
from the heart of praCh,
comes this "art of faCt."

from : " DALAMA...the lost chapter."
traX : # 19   (copy right 2003)
reprinted with permission of the author

The Great EsCape!
PraCh

i was born in a hut,
umbilical cord cut.
a lil bit torned up,
when the big storm erupt.
it muddied the sand,
and flooded the land,
rain drops through roof top,
had to use pots and pans.
drown the town into a lake.
i had a close encounter
with a venomous snake.
i was deep asleep
it was wide awake.
all it take was one bite,
my life would have ended that day.
but it went away,
so on earth i was kept.
already facing death,
before i even took my first step.
and worst yet,
threats surrounds us.
even though i was a new born,
innocent like a unicorn,
i'd die too if the Khmer Rouge found us.
bombs burst, the land to bits.
and people disappear like they never exist.
nobody ask questions,

"The Great EsCape!"   101

they afraid they'll be next.
so many rumors, nobody wanna say shit.
there's even story about a massive grave pit.
love our land to death, but can't stay no longer.
our only chance is make it...
across the border.

watch out !
for booby traps and land mines,
ain't no time to take breaks.
death is close behind,
night or day it's not OK!
gotta stay awake!
no matter what it take,
we gotta make,
"The Great EsCape!"

we take, wait.
in past tense we took.
valuable belongings
wrapped it up with sheets.
a pair of pot and pans,
so we can cook food to eat.
take what weight we can carry,
and leave the rest behind.
we had to move fast,
what we didn't have was time.
we wasn't the only ones,
there were hundreds upon thousands,
young and old men
and women and children,
swimming into the mountains.
look'n for hope,
like fishes searching for water.
our mission was crossing
over Thailand border.
we ran out of food,

102 *Modern Literature of Cambodia*

eat what we could find.
plus we had to watch our steps,
for booby traps and land mines.
thirsty no water, we had to drink rain.
it got to the point,
where we need blood,
just to pump the vein, the pain,
when there's total silence,
you know danger ahead.
and when the bomb goes off,
then you know some one's dead.
but forward ahead,
each step takes us closer,
we gotta make it across the border.
we lost our hearts,
but found the strength in our souls,
words can't describe,
but the stories must be told.
it's hard to forget
what we went through.
the woods, the jungles,
the fields of death.
the struggles continue,
but we're gonna make it!

watch out!
for booby traps and land mines
ain't no time to take breaks.
death is close behind,
night or day, it's not OK!
gotta stay awake!
no matter what it takes,
we gotta make...
"The Great EsCape!"

from : Dalama..."the lost chapter."
traX : # 6 (2003)
Republished with permission of the author

Kelley Pheng is a Cambodian-American spoken word artist and community activist who was born in Modesto, California, on April 10, 1989. She is a graduate of CSU Long Beach with a major in Psychology. Kelley uses spoken word as an outlet for her experience of growing up with the dual identity of being Cambodian and American and to tell the stories of her parents' and relatives' struggles coming to and surviving in America. She sees spoken word and poetry as a way to express both her own experience and that of the Cambodian community.

Hystory of a DREAM

[Descendant of Refugees' Elevation from Ambition to a Mission]
Kelley Peng

I was 23 with no college degree
Typical of me to be a young American
Paper-chasin'
Instead of chasin' dreams,
Aspirations,
Ambitions.
Living a life with no mission
And forgetting the one my parents had given.

But this world we live in
Raised me to only believe in
Being what they saw fit for me.
The term 'Southeast Asian' was a mystery
And even worse, 'Cambodian' was not in their vocabulary.
School textbooks made no mention of our Hystory
And I was told to suppress my Cambodian identity.

I was told to suppress what they didn't want me to be
It was like I did not exist.
I felt like nothing.
I felt worthless.
But they didn't understand the stress

Of my family.
They couldn't fathom growing up with parents torn apart
by PTSD
Coming from a country torn apart by war.
Even I fail to grasp the realities of their past
And the pain of their present.
Of how they continue to live in nightmares
But nobody else cares.
Only I do.
And even in my wildest dreams,
I could never imagine the things that they've seen
So I wonder,
Did they ever dream?

Did my father dream when he was tied up in chains?
Did he think he'd be able to endure the pain
And see the light of day again?
Did he know he'd make it to see today?
That he'd be able to live by the beautiful Bay
That he'd be able to support a family of 6 with an AA?
Did he dream that through the torture, there is a life after
That through him his children would only know laughter?

Did my mother dream when she became the only one left?
After her family was taken and put to death
After her first born passed in her arms
After all the destruction and harm
Did she still have faith that she'd make it on her own?
That she'd be able to build herself another home
That she'd find herself with me, another daughter
Did she dream that one day, she would no longer have to
witness the slaughter?

Did my sister dream that she'd survive?
That somehow, she'd manage to be alive,
And escape with our mother from that jungle she was born into
And celebrate all that they had been through?

"Hystory of a DREAM" 105

Would she have?
If she had survived?

But instead, she died.
And our mother mourned.
In my sister's place, I was born.
But in my place, her spirit lives on
Because I am the culmination of all these things
Their dreams
Their nightmares
Their visions have become my mission
That stepping onto this soil was never the end of a struggle
That being in this country didn't mean the end of a hustle
That being alive meant more than just living
That having 'DREAMS' meant more than just dreaming.

So here I am
A young Cambodian-American.
A college student at 24
With nothing more than what they've given me
With a degree bestowed upon me by no university
Because I am built by degrees of what it means to be
The blood of Angkorian ancestry,
A proud descendant of Cambodian refugees.

A Play
by
Cambodian Americans

The Unraveling Truth:
A Play in Four Acts
Written by Malain Houmoeung, Peter Duong, and Sitavy Thorng

This bilingual play was performed at the Carpenter Center at CSU Long Beach on March 17, 2013. The transliteration system for the Cambodian was established by the writers.

<u>Plot</u>
A Cambodian refugee family now living in America struggles to understand the past. Through a contemporary Cambodian tale of strife, sacrifice and a bit of magical intervention, this family finally faces a brighter future together.

<u>Character List and Roles</u>
American Story
Narrator
Mother, Sothy Seim
Father, Buly Seim
Older Sister, Sorany Seim
Younger Sister, Somaly Seim
Younger Brother, Danny Seim
Mysterious Grandma

Cambodian folktale
Hero, Mak Terung/Tung
King
Village beauty, Muy Juy
King's messanger, Ding Ding/ A Ding Ding
Villagers
Soldiers
Wise man

108 *Modern Literature of Cambodia*

ACT 1, Scene 1

(The curtain opens with spotlight on center stage. The scene is a simple living room.)

Sothy: *(Screaming)* Honey, I never argue with you or ask for anything. I've been faithful to you.

Buly: *(Drunk)* Don't talk too much. I don't want to talk. Give me something to eat. Hurry!

Sothy: *(Throws food at Buly's feet)* Hungry? *(Exasperated)* Hungry? Here! Eat until your mouth is full!

Buly: Why'd you throw it for? Don't forget what I did for you! Don't forget who saved your life!

Sothy: You think that I don't know?! That's the reason why I loved you faithfully. And, do you even love me? Say it for once…

(The lights dim with only the stage front still lit. Sothy walks into the light.)

Sothy: *(Addressing the audience)* I don't know what to do. I wouldn't think it would be this hard. I really do love him, but I don't know if I can take this anymore. He saved my life and I am forever grateful, but *(pause)* now do I have a life?

(Stage goes dark while more living room props are moved on stage.)

ACT 1, Scene 2

(The stage is dimly lit. There is a table stage left and more living room props than in Scene 1. Danny, Somaly, and Sorany are positioned from stage right to left; Buly and Sothy are far stage left. They are acting silently as the narrator speaks.)

"The Unraveling Truth"   109

Narrator: _(Offstage)_ The relationship between Sothy and Buly has slowly started to grow apart, but they believe that it is better to have each other than no one at all. After several years, Buly and Sothy have settled down and now have three children named Sorany, Somaly, and Danny.

(The stage is dark; slowly the lights come on, full stage. The family is together in the same room but each character is doing their own thing. The characters Danny, Somaly and Sorany are positioned under spot lights from stage right to stage left. As they speak, the light illuminates them one by one, starting with Sorany and ending with Danny.)

Sorany: _(Speaks to the audience)_ Sorany is the name that my parents gave me. You see these two people; they are my parents. They just happen to be together. By just looking at my parent's relationship, I don't believe in love.

Somaly: _(Addressing audience)_ Do you guys believe in love? One day, my heart will _(sighing sound while smiling)_ go to that special person _(pauses and then points into the audience)_. YOU! There in the audience, do you feel what I feel? I want to feel that unexplainable feeling where I am content. I know love is out there, and I will show my parents that love can still exist if they give it another chance. If only ... _(cut off by Danny)._

Danny: _(Speaking to the audience)_ IT'S MY TURN! Hi guys, what's up. I'm Danny. Unlike my sisters, I spend most of my time playing video games _(he pauses and looks a little sad)_ to try and escape the dysfunction of my family. _(Slight pause)_ It's. . . whatever.

(After Danny sits back down, full lights on stage right. Sothy walks into the living room carrying groceries and sees Danny

110   *Modern Literature of Cambodia*

on the floor playing video games.)

Sothy:	Danny, oh Danny, help me put the food away. *(Danny does not hear his mom at first.)*
Sothy:	You pestered ears! *Mak* said come here!
Danny:	Okay! Okay! I'm coming! (*but continues to play the video game*).

(Sothy rapidly walks towards Danny. She violently dumps the groceries on the floor. She struggles to undo her belt, but can't; then turns to the nearest random object to use as a threat.)

Sothy:	Ugh! This boy. Get your butt off the ground. Get up now! Stop being lazy! Day after day, all you do is play that *Call of Dooty*! You know when I was your age, I work hard! I never lazy! I studied hard and earn good grades. I work in field all day until sun go down.
Danny:	*(Speaks quietly but loud enough for Sothy to hear)* Yet you can't help me with my homework.

(Somaly walks in, stands and watches as she shakes her head.)

Sothy:	*(Makes a funny sound in Khmer)* What did you say? I kick you, boy! Yeuhhhh!...
Somaly:	Danny, just go and help mom. She's going to keep nagging at you until you do it.
Danny:	Why don't you do it? You are standing right there. I'm almost at level fourteen! Besides, you need to stop watching K-dramas. It's not like you have a hot guy wanting you any time soon! *(Laughs.)*
Somaly:	Why you little… You're such a little brat! *(She gets cut off by Buly.)*
Buly:	What's the ruckus? Listen, I work morning

"The Unraveling Truth"   111

until night to raise you guys. When it's night, that's when I rest. If you want to be loud then go somewhere else!

(Sorany starts to pace angrily.)

Sorany: I can never study in this house! It's hardly ever quiet with everybody arguing. I'm leaving!

Buly: *(In Khmer) Tha mech? (In English)* What'd you say?! Do you know how much I sacrificed to get you where you are right now? You have a home, so stay home!

Sorany: *Ba*, don't act like *Mak* didn't do anything. At least she raised us.

Buly: *(Pauses)* Ugh, I don't want to deal with this. Ugh, these kids, I'm going to turn crazy.

(Sothy watches Buly walk out and feels guilty. She quietly leaves the stage.)

Danny: That's it. Imma go back and finish level fourteen.

Somaly: Danny stop, we need to talk about this. Aren't you tired of Ma and Pa fighting? Why can't we be like... like...those American families? The ones that eat dinner together everyday!

Sorany: That's because the media is fake. Not all families are like that, Somaly. Don't you get it? Life isn't fair.

(Sothy walks in and hears the children talking.)

Somaly: Life isn't fair because we don't do anything about it. All we do is argue and yelling doesn't solve anything. I really don't want my future husband to suffer and be a part of this family. We need to change things around here.

Danny: You and your fantasies, Somaly. Sooner or later,

112   *Modern Literature of Cambodia*

> all of this is not going to matter. We are going to
> move out someday and forget about this family.

Somaly: But *(pause)* we can't leave mom like this
because **all of this** is still going to matter to her.

(Stage lights fade out.)

ACT 1, Scene 3

(Lights on center stage. Buly walks in drunk and angry. Sothy comes out hesitantly. Actors walk towards the light.)

Sothy: Did you go out drinking again? Ugh, when are
you going to wake up and realize what you're
doing?

Buly: What is there to eat?

Sothy: *Bong*! Listen to me! I put up with this too long!
I'm trying and trying *(gets cut off by Buly).*

Buly: You?! You put up with me?! I have to put up with
you!   Can't take it? I am the reason why we are
under this roof! Let me tell you, I can leave you
anytime.

Sothy: Well. Go ahead and leave. Why haven't you left
then?

Buly: *(Speaking In Khmer, he flips the chair violently.)*
WHY HAVEN'T I LEFT?

(The children hear them arguing and peer out to see.)

Sothy: *(Speaking in English)* You see?! You can't
respond because you don't know.

Buly: You want to try me? If you don't shut your
mouth, I'll teach you.

Sothy: If you want to hit me, hit me. It wouldn't be the
only time you have hurt me!

(Buly, angered by what Sothy has said, loses control and

"The Unraveling Truth" 113

attempts to hit her. The children react in time before he strikes her.)

Somaly and Danny: *(Shout together to intervene)* STOP!

(Full stage lights on. Somaly runs to shield Sothy. Danny attempts to stop Buly from hitting her. Sorany walks slowly on stage distraught and faces Buly, looking directly into his eyes.)

Sorany: You can never be a good father to us. You will never be a man for mom. Get out.

(Buly is shocked by what Sorany has said to him. He pushes Danny to the side and storms halfway up stage right. Sorany remains in the same place, angry, facing as if Buly was still standing there. Sothy collapses to the ground while Somaly tries to help her. Danny is on his knees angry and ready to cry. Stage lights slowly fade out.)

ACT 1, Scene 4

(The stage is lit but with a creepy, greenish light.)

Narrator: *(Offstage)* Buly is angered by how his family has treated him. As he storms out of the house, he bumps into an old lady in the street.

Buly: A ghost! Help me, a ghost is haunting me!

Grandma: I'm not a ghost, grandchild *(evil, ugly laugh).*

Buly: I deeply apologize, grandma.

(The old grandmother looks at him in a very strange way, touches him and reads his mental and physical state.)

Grandma: You are very lucky to live but you are not living. You must fix that or something bad will happen.

114   *Modern Literature of Cambodia*

Come closer.

Narrator: Grandma pulls him closer and starts chanting and mumbling. Buly is confused and weirded out by the situation and runs off.

(Lights fade out.)

ACT 1, Scene 5

(The stage is split into two scenes. Sothy is sitting at a table, stage right. Stage right is brightly lit, stage left is dim. After Sorany enters stage right, the light fades. Sothy is now sobbing.)

Sorany: Ma?

Sothy: *(Quickly wipes away tears)* Oh, Sorany. What happen? You can't sleep?

Sorany: *(Walks to the table and sits down. She places a hand on her mother.)* Ma, are you crying?

Sothy: *(Khmer and English)* No *koun*. I'm not crying. I just can't sleep right now.

Sorany: Ma. Why are you still with dad? He is hurting our family too much. Why can't you just leave him?

Sothy: Don't worry about it, daughter. Just go back to sleep. Mom is okay.

Sorany: No, ma. I'm going to stay up with you to make sure you are okay. I can't sleep knowing that you are like this. You shouldn't be alone right now *(long pause of hesitation)*. Ma, how can you even love this man?

Sothy: *Koun, (sigh)* at the end of the day, he is still and always will be your father. You need to respect him and love him *(pause)*. You know *(pause)* your dad and I . . . we weren't always like this.

Sorany: Really? What happened?

"The Unraveling Truth" 115

Sothy: Love is not the same for everyone. Sit here, *koun,* I want to share with you a story about love and its unraveling truth.

(Stage lights off.)

<u>ACT 2, Scene 1</u>

(Stage is fully lit on a traditional Cambodian market scene.)

Narrator: *(Offstage)* During this time, Ou Bong Province was beautiful and peaceful. There was much prosperity throughout the land and life was as charming as could be. Even more beautiful, was a young couple madly in love. The whole village knew of the passion and love this couple felt for one another. The two go by the name of Mak Tung and Muy Juy.

(Mak Tung and Muy Juy, dressed as villagers, enter together carrying baskets on their heads.)

Mak Tung: Honey, are you tired? Do you want to stop and rest?

Muy Juy: Yes, *bong.* You must be tired too. Let's take a little break under that tree over there.

Mak Tung: *Oun,* make sure you rest well. You may fall from the sky, you may fall from a tree, but the best way to fall . . . is in love with me!

(He gets really close and tries to touch her face. She slaps away his hand, touches her face, and walks away smiling.)

Muy Juy: [Khmer] Yee, bong gom prohurn pek. Proyat diy gabot, and you won't have a hand anymore.
(She smiles) Hey, don't misbehave!

Mak Tung: Oh, honey . . . I know you could NEVER hurt me. You LOVE me too much.

116 *Modern Literature of Cambodia*

Muy Juy: Are you so sure *bong*? Love makes you do crazy things *(she giggles)*.

Mak Tung: I know true love does make you do crazy things. That's why there is one thing I have to ask you.

Muy Juy: What is it *bong*? You look so serious… is everything okay?

Mak Tung: No, everything isn't okay. There is something that I have to get off of my chest and it will be life changing.

Muy Juy: What is it *bong*?! Are you unhappy? Is your health okay?

Mak Tung: My health isn't okay because I no longer have a heart. It belongs to you. And what I wanted to say is . . . Will you marry me *oun* Muy Juy?

Muy Juy: *(She's shocked and drops what she is holding. She turns away nervously, then turns back smiling.)* Yes, *Bong*. I have been waiting for this day. *(They hug and embrace affectionately; traditional Khmer music starts playing; lights fade out).*

ACT 2, Scene 2

Narrator: *(Offstage)* Love knows no limits or boundaries. We simply accept the love we think we deserve. The village of Ou Bong is bustling with excitement and joy since the villagers know the great news about the engagement of Muy Juy and Mak Tung. Laughing and embracing, the villagers have gathered together to celebrate the love that these two share by watching a performance of the Blessing Dance.

(Full stage lights; Blessing Dance is performed.)

INTERMISSION

"The Unraveling Truth" 117

(Scene continues; curtain opens to villagers stage right with the King and Ding Ding stage left.)

Narrator: *(Offstage)* The king was on a stroll around the village when he heard the sound of celebration and joy. He became curious and wanted to know what sort of celebration could be this big.

King: Hey, A Ding Ding! Go check on what is happening over there.

Ding Ding: Yes, your Highness. I go see for you what is going on!

(Ding Ding rushes over to see; wobbling, he trips and falls on his bottom as he arrives. He clears his throat.)

Ding Ding: Hey, you all! What are you doing here? My King is here! He wants to know!

Villagers: *(Seeming shocked to hear about the King. They speak in unison)* King?!

(Then immediately all the villagers kneel to the ground in a gesture of respect.)

King: A DING DING! What is taking so long over there!?!?

Ding Ding: YES, COMING!!!

(As Ding Ding rushes back, the King walks through the village acting like a big man, observing everyone. He suddenly stops. He sees a beautiful woman in the line of villagers and rubs his chin. The King turns around and smiles at the audience. Then Muy Juy and he make eye contact, but she looks away quickly. The front of the center stage is brightly lit.)

King: *(Addressing the audience from front center stage)* I am a handsome and powerful king. I rule this entire kingdom and I still need to find a

118   *Modern Literature of Cambodia*

woman to reign with me. I can have any of you beautiful women out there. But I already have someone in mind.

(Stage lights off.)

ACT 2, Scene 3

(The setting is nighttime with the sound of crickets chirping. Muy Juy and Mak Tung are sound asleep close to each other. The stage is infused in a dark blue color with a dimly lit center stage. Muy Juy is tossing and turning; she then wakes up from a terrible dream.)

Muy Juy: *(She screams)* AHHHHH!!!!

(Then crying and sobbing, she reaches for Mak Tung so he can comfort her in his arms. The center stage is now fully lit. Mak Tung wakes up startled by Muy Juy.)

Mak Tung: *OUN! OUN!* What's wrong!?
Muy Juy: *Bong*! I had the worst dream! I had a dream that there was a king serpent. He hurt you *(pause)*. He clawed out your eyes and left you to die *(pause)*. I, I *(pause)* was so helpless. He then came to me *(pause)* and. . . and (pause) he took me away . . .
Mak Tung: *(Leans to hug her and caresses her hair)* Oun, it's okay. It's just a dream. No one will take you away. As long as I'm here, no one will hurt you. I will be here. I promise.
Muy Juy: *(Acts very frightened) Bong* it was so scary. It felt so real. I don't ever want to leave you.
Mak Tung: It's okay, *oun*. Just go back to sleep.

(He sings gently to put her back to sleep. After she falls asleep, Mak Tung steps outside their sleeping area. The backstage lighting is dim while the center front stage is brightly

lit.)

Mak Tung: *(Speaks to the audience from center front stage.)* That dream *(pause)* could it be true? Something doesn't feel right, but can something really happen between me and Muy Juy? I have never loved anyone so much. I won't let anything happen to her. Otherwise, I will never forgive myself if something happens to Muy Juy.

(The stage lights fades out as Mak Tung looks back at her.)

ACT 2, Scene 4

(Village scene with full stage lights.)

Narrator: *(Offstage)* Muy Juy and Mak Tung knew that the dream was a sign that something could happen. But both believed that showing fear would only cause each other to worry. The next morning, Muy Juy and Mak Tung go about their day as if nothing has happened.

(A busy village scene is underway. Muy Juy walks toward front stage and meets Mak Tung as he is leaving to help with the harvest in another village.)

Muy Juy: Good morning, *bong*, I packed some rice and dried fish for you. You need all the energy you can get in order to help with the harvest.

Mak Tung: *Akun* [thank you], *oun.* You sure know how to make your man's stomach happy with your delicious *prahok* and *trey ngeet*! I promise I will be back in no time. Take care of yourself, okay? Remember, nothing will happen to you as long as I am here.

Muy Juy: I will, *bong*. I love you so much. Please be safe

120   *Modern Literature of Cambodia*

and return to me as soon as possible.

(Mak Tung and Muy Juy embrace and say their farewells. Muy Juy is interacting with the villagers while the King walks on stage and Mak Tung departs. As Muy Juy and the King walk towards each other, she accidently stumbles into him.)

King: Hey, where do you think you're going? *(He steps in front of her every time she tries to move around him.)*

Muy Juy: Excuse me, King. I must get to the village to sell my products.

King: Hey! Hey! Hey! Now, why are you in such a rush? Don't you want to spend time with me?

Muy Juy: *(Looking at him in disgust and rolling her eyes)* Excuse me, your majesty, but I must be on my way *(she tries to dart past him).*

King;   *(Grabbing her arm)* Hey! Not so fast! You are a beautiful girl. Are you single?

Muy Juy: *(Stops and kneels in respect)* I'm sorry, your Majesty, but it is not appropriate for you to treat a woman this way. Maybe that's why YOU'RE SINGLE. Please let me go.

King: *(Watches Muy Juy walk away)* I will be back for you. You can be sure of that.

(The stage lights dim as the King's servants leave the stage.)

ACT 3, Scene 1

(The entire stage is fully lit for a live market scene. Muy Juy is selling perfume when the king's soldiers enter the village and surround her.)

Muy Juy: *(Sounding distressed)* What is going on here?!

Soldier 1: The King has ordered your arrest because you

"The Unraveling Truth" **121**

	assaulted him.
Muy Juy:	ASSULTED HIM? IN WHAT WAY? Unhand me this instant!
Soldier 1:	Arrest her!

(A soldier ties her hands behind her back and pushes her down to her knees. The King silently walks over, standing before her smirking.)

King:	I told you I'd be back for you. Now, because you have assaulted me, the King *(pause),* I believe there is a punishment for those who lay hands on royalty. But I suppose there is a way to avoid the punishment that you deserve.
Muy Juy:	*(Struggling and restless)* And what is that?
King:	I understand that you are with a certain somebody. Ah, Meka Tron[1].
Muy Juy:	His name is MAK TERUNG!
King:	Ga-zun-tite. Let me make a deal with you. You will marry me and in return, Meka Tron's life will be spared. If you choose not to marry me, your punishment is to witness his death.
Muy Juy:	*(Devastated, teary eyed, and feeling helpless)* You can't do this!
King:	*(Unsympathetic)* I am aware that, ah, Meka Tron . . .
Muy Juy:	*(Shouting)* MAK TERUNG!
King:	*(Pausing with a slight smirk)* Mak Terung has gone to another village. It will be sad if he couldn't come home *(pausing and smirking again).* It would be really sad if he couldn't say even one last word to you.

(Muy Juy struggles to escape so that she can hurt the king,

---

[1] A funny reference in Cambodian to the Transformers

122 *Modern Literature of Cambodia*

but she is strongly restrained.)

King: I can easily order my men to . . .
Muy Juy: *(Shouting)* NO! I will do it. I will marry you. Just don't lay a single finger on Mak Terung!
King: *(With an evil smile)* Men! Take my bride to the royal palace. We have a wedding to plan.

(Stage lights off.)

ACT 3, Scene 2

(The center stage is dimly lit. A hut is set up center stage.)

Narrator: *(Offstage)* Mak Tung never thought that he would return to an empty home. Devastated, he searched the whole village hoping to hear that sweet voice of Muy Juy. Villagers hearing his call for her are afraid to bring him the bad news. Soon, they can no longer take his broken heart and tell him what happened.
Mak Tung: *(Distraught)* I promised Muy Juy. I promised that nothing bad would happen to her *(pause)* as long as I am beside her. *(He screams)* WHY DID I LEAVE THE VILLAGE?! There are hundreds of beautiful women in this village, and the King had to chose Muy Juy? I will not rest until Muy Juy and I are together again. I won't.

(The villagers enter stage right.)

Villager 1: *(Addresses Mak Tung)* Mak Tung, the village can no longer take the loss of Muy Juy. We are saddened to see the love you two shared be ripped apart. Your love for Muy Juy brought light to our village and hope to those who wish to find true love. That is why we all agree to fight for Muy Juy's freedom. We are in for a battle.

(Mak Tung gets up and hugs Villager 1 and thanks the rest of the villagers. The stage lights go off and the curtain closes.)

ACT 3, Scene 3

Narrator: *(Offstage)* It is the day of the King and Muy Juy's wedding. The kingdom is filled with joy and celebration for their future queen. Everyone but Muy Juy is happy as dances are performed to bring good luck to the new couple.

(Curtain opens; full stage lights as a dance is performed. After the dance, stage lights off and the curtains close. Curtains open to a split stage setting: on stage right is an unlit village scene; stage left is a palace setting fully lit.)

Muy Juy: *(In the palace and distraught)* Am I going to have to marry the King? Mak Tung promised me that he would be by my side. I just hope he gets here in time. I would rather die than marry the King.

(Stage left, light dims; stage right, full lighting on a village scene.)

Mak Tung: *(Addressing the villagers)* I want to thank you all for fighting beside me. You all know very well that life has no meaning without Muy Juy. I am eternally grateful for each and every one of you, and I do not know how I can repay you all.

Villager 2:   There is no need to repay us. As long as Muy Juy is back in this village, our life is as good as before.

Villager 3:   Yes, Muy Juy is one of us. Loosing her would be the missing piece of our village. Without her, how are we all going to smell good without perfumes?

Villager 4:   That is why we plan to attack as soon as the second dance ends. The girl I love is performing

124   *Modern Literature of Cambodia*

in that dance, and I don't want to waste the effort and time she has put into the performance.

(The light shifts to left stage after Villager 4 speaks. Muy Juy is seated, waiting to be called to the wedding.)

Mak Tung: Ha! ha! It is settled. We will attack right after the second dance. Now, let us walk right into battle and bring back the one I am destined to marry!

Villagers: *(Yelling together in Khmer)* Justice will be served! *(The villagers cheer. As they are yelling, Muy Juy reacts as if she has heard them, but it is only a servant who has called her out to the dance performance.)*

(Stage lights out and curtains close.)

ACT 3, Scene 4

Narrator: *(Offstage)* Ladies and gentlemen! May I have your attention please? I welcome you to the ceremony when the King will finally be wed to the beautiful Muy Juy. Please enjoy this next performance as the dancers wish good luck and prosperity for our King and future Queen!

(Curtains open, stage full lights, to a palace setting and the performance of the Coconut Dance. Stage lights go off at the end of the dance then on again as the King and Muy Juy enter stage left.)

King: *(In Khmer)* It's time, beautiful. *(In English)* I promise you that a life with me will be full of luxury rather than being with a low-life rat like Mak Terung. COME!

Muy Juy: *(Close to sobbing)* You will never be half the

"The Unraveling Truth"   125

man that Mak Terung is. Mark my words, money can NEVER buy love.

(The King and Muy Juy exit stage right. The scene continues with comic relief. The villagers enter stage left, running boisterously for the battle until they realize they are in the wrong area. They quickly exit stage left. Then the King and Muy Juy enter stage right. Mak Tung appears on stage left.)

Muy Juy: *(Yells as she sees him)* MAK TERUNG.

Mak Tung: *(Speaks forcefully to the King)* I'm here to take my bride Muy Juy back! And I am not leaving until she is in my arms again!

King: *(Arrogantly)* You think you can come into my kingdom as if you own the place? And what's this?! You brought your little village rats with you?

Mak Tung: *(Speaking strongly)* I will do whatever it takes to get my Muy Juy back. Even if it means fighting you to the death!

King: *(Sarcastically)* You think you and your little villagers can take down my soldiers? *(He gestures to his soldiers.)* We'll see about that. If it's a battle you want! It's a battle you'll get!

(Battle scene with music, sword fighting, and fog. Stage lights off at end of battle.)

ACT 3, Scene 5

(Center stage light on; backstage lighting dim. Villagers and soldiers are spread out on the floor, wounded. The King has grabbed Mak Tung by the shirt and is holding a knife to his throat as Muy Juy watches in despair.)

Muy Juy: *(Pleading)* Please, your Highness. Don't hurt Mak Tung. It doesn't have to be this way.

126   *Modern Literature of Cambodia*

King: *(Angrily)* You love this piece of trash that much? I gave you everything, and you still don't see me as a good man.

Mak Tung: That's because you can't force someone to love you.

King: Silence! I'm not talking to you!

Muy Juy: Please. I will marry you just as long as you let Mak Tung go!

(The King is angrily holding onto Mak Tung's shirt.)

Muy Juy: *(Speaking desperately)* Get off of him! *(She pushes the King away from Mak Tung, whom she then hugs and embraces.)*

King: You love him so much! You won't love him anymore if he's dead!

(The background lighting turns red. The King charges to stab Mak Tung, but Muy Juy jumps in front of him just as the King thrusts his knife. It goes through Muy Juy, barely touching Mak Tung. She collapses, as the light fades to a reddish pink.)

Muy Juy: *(Barely breathing) Bong*, I have never loved anyone as much as you. Even if in this life we are not meant to be together, I know we will meet again. Thank you for letting me know what true love feels like. Love knows no limits and you accept the love you deserve. I accept love enough to sacrifice my life. I love you, *bong (she closes her eyes and dies).*

Mak Tung: *(Screaming)* MUY JUY! Muy Juy stay with me! MUY JUY, DON'T LEAVE! No *(sobbing)*. Please. I'm here now. Nothing bad can happen to you. Muy Juy, *oun*. Stay with me!

(The stage lights slowly fade. The stage is quickly transformed to a modern living room setting.)

"The Unraveling Truth" 127

<u>ACT 4, Scene 1</u>

(Lights go up to dim. Back in the living room, Sothy and Sorany are in the same position as before. Danny is comically imitating the fighting scene. Somaly is fantasizing about her own version of the folktale. Sorany, who is not impressed by the folktale, questions why someone would die for another because of love.)

Narrator: *(Offstage)* Love is defined for those who have understood and experienced its meaning. Love is unexpected. Love is an adventure. Today, finding love, especially true love, is difficult. Those that fight and exceed their limit know that true love is a privilege. And once you find love, you want to hold it close to your heart.

(Bright light goes on stage right.)

Sothy: You see, *koun*, love makes you do crazy things. You wonder why I am still with your dad. It's not only because he saved my life, but . . .
(Sothy is cut off).

Somaly: *Mak*, you always mention that *Ba* saved your life. But you never explain it.

(Sothy does not want to tell her children that she has a fatal heart condition.)

Sothy: Children, it is better to have one parent than none at all.

Sorany: *(Puzzled and a little annoyed because of her mother not answering her directly)* Why are you talking to me like something is going to happen to you?

(Lights on full stage.)

128 *Modern Literature of Cambodia*

Buly: *(Walks in angrily, is aggressive, and throwing things)* Why can no one respect me in this house huh?! Why is life so harsh to me!? Why is there no good in my life?! Why . . . *(gets cut off)*.

(Somaly runs to Buly and tries to stop him.)

Somaly: Just drop it, please. Pa, please, I beg you, stop.

(Buly pushes her to the side. Danny runs to help Somaly. Sorany gets up rapidly and charges for Buly when Sothy interrupts her.)

Sothy: STOP IT, NOW! My heart cannot take... *(Overwhelmed she collapses to the floor)*.

(Danny and Somaly run to Sothy.)

Danny: *Mak*! Call 911! Hurry, *loeurn*!

(Buly is in shock and can't move.)

Sorany: *(Looks at Sothy and then at Buly. Angry and blaming Buly, she speaks)* You will NOT go near her.
Danny: HURRY UP AND CALL 911!

(Lights fade slowly to complete darkness while Somaly rushes to the telephone.)

Somaly: I'm calling, I'm calling!

(The stage is dark; the sound of a phone ringing.)

Narrator: *(Offstage)* 911, what's your emergency?

"The Unraveling Truth"   129

(In the background, there are sounds of the family sobbing for Sothy. They are trying to wake her up.)

Narrator: *(Offstage)* Hello? Hello? 911, what's your emergency?

(There is the sound of a telephone being hung up.)

<u>ACT 4, Scene 2</u>

(Lights go up dimly to reveal the family in their home having a memorial service for Sothy. Incense is burning. They are praying at Sothy's memorial shrine. Lights on stage right. There is about five seconds of silence, then Sothy's name is keened. Buly starts breaking down as he looks at his wife's memorial shrine again.)

Somaly: *(In a tearful voice)* Mom, I hope you are in a better place right now. I miss you so much. Please watch over us.

Danny: *(Speaking tragically)* I'm sorry for being lazy and talking back, *Mak*. I should have helped you with the groceries, but I was so stupid. I'll try to change and be a better man, *Mak (crying).*

(Buly bursts out crying hysterically and touches the shrine. Sorany slowly gets up and stands.)

Sorany: *(Angrily)* You have no right to cry. Dad, you have no right to cry in front of mom!

(Sorany turns towards the door and gradually heads that direction.)

Buly: *(Sadly, referring to himself)* Dad, is sorry.

Sorany: For what? For hurting my mom? For making her stay with you because she owes you? You didn't

130   *Modern Literature of Cambodian*

save her life, you kept her just to save
yourself from your own troubles!

(A video with scenes of the Khmer Rouge and civil war plays on a back screen while Buly acts out the past on the other side of the stage. Stage left, the light is still bright. Stage right is dimly lit.)

Buly: *(Pleading)* Listen to dad for a moment. I really did save her, but she did the same for me. *Mak* never told you... but I was forced to be a *teihien* [soldier] for the Khmer Rouge. *(Stage left, light dims)* I was ordered to destroy the *phum* [village] where your mother lived. She was one of the last people to live, and I was ordered to kill her.

Sorany: *(In a monotone)* What made you stop?

Buly: *(In a sorrowful voice)* Something about her, when I first saw her, made me feel human again. And all those sins I committed as a soldier, she made me feel forgiven.

(Light goes off stage right.)

Somaly: *(In a sad but accusing voice)* All these family secrets about my own parents were kept from your own daughter. Dad, do you know how long we wanted to know about what happened to you guys?

Sorany;   *(Forcefully)* Let's go guys; we're leaving. We're going to live at Grandma's house.

Danny;   *(Hysterical)* No! I want to stay with Pa! *(Pulling and begging his father)* Pa, please can I live with you? I promise I'll be a good son. I'll stop playing games. My mom is gone, I need my dad. Don't treat me like an orphan child.

(Buly has his head bowed, ashamed.)

"The Unraveling Truth"   131

Danny: Can I, dad? *(pause)*. DAD! *(Turns to Sorany and Somaly on his knees now, pleading)* Please, *bong*, I'll be good! Can I stay here? I'll be good. I'll stop playing video games.

Somaly;   *(In a firm but concerned voice)* Listen to *bong*, we're living at *yeay's* [grandmother's] house. We have to stick together, okay Ga-bi [the nickname of the youngest sibling]? *(She touches his head)* It's going to be all right.

Somaly: *(Somaly turns to Buly, concerned but firm)* Take care of yourself. Cut back on rice and don't use too much fish sauce in your food. Your cholesterol and sodium levels are high. Bye, dad. This will be the last time.

(She kneels on the floor in order to properly bow to her father and then gets up. Sorany and Somaly struggle to pull Danny out of the room; they drag him off stage right.)

Sorany: Stop being stubborn, Ga-bi! Danny, are your ears stuffed again? Let's go!

(Red and purple lights start flickering and fog filters across the stage. The lights all go off, then a red light shines on Buly who is in a subconscious state.)

ACT 4, Scene 3

(The stage is lit with a dark red light. The pre-recorded voices of Buly, the old grandmother and Sothy play. Then the stage goes dark. There is the sound of a tin can being repeatedly struck).

ACT 4, Scene 4

(The setting has returned to the original family scene in ACT I, Scene 3. Buly is standing with the mysterious old grand-mother as she tells his future. Right stage, lights dim; left

132 *Modern Literature of Cambodia*

stage, full lights. There is a door in the middle of the stage separating it into two sides.)

Narrator: *(Offstage)* Buly has fully returned to a conscious state. He realizes what can happen in his future if he doesn't learn to love his wife, children and himself.

Buly: *(Having an epiphany, he is breathing heavily while still in shock.)* OH MY GOODNESS GRACIOUS!!!

Grandma: *(In an old creaky voice)* That's all that *Look Yeay* has for today, *na jaov*. Go home to where you belong and make things right.

Buly: *(Looking humbled)* Yes, *Look Yeay*. Thank you very much, *Look Yeay (He bows to her in the most respectful way).*

(Once the old grandmother has exited stage right, the light goes off. The light comes on stage left as soon as Buly goes through the door into the scene of his home. Buly sees his children.)

Buly: Ah *tr'jeak thlong*! [Stuffed ears].
Danny: *(Scared) Bhat* [Yes], *Pa!*

(Looking stronger, Buly motions with his hand for Danny to approach him.)

Buly: *Meek nih, phleam* (come here, now!) You *A Peouv* [youngest child], but you da man. Be strong for your *Mak* and your *bong*s.

(Buly grabs and hugs Danny in the manliest way possible. Sorany and Somaly walk into the room from stage left, assuming there is more trouble. Buly sees Somaly and then grabs and hugs her.)

"The Unraveling Truth"   133

Buly: Somaly, study hard. Stay away from boys, OK?! You watch too much K-dramas. Boy crazy, no good!

Somaly: PAAA!! *(Embarrassed, she looks at Danny like she wants to kill him for telling her dad.)* You told him?! *(She moves like she's going to punch her brother.)*

Buly: *(Turns to speak to Sorany)* You are the eldest and you take care of the family. Go to school, study hard, and make a lot of da money for dad to spend. Dad is just kidding. Put YOU first, love will come find you later. Proud of you, my *koun thom* [eldest child].

Sorany: Yes, Dad.

(They both gradually break the ice and finally hug. Buly is curious about his wife.)

Buly: Where is Mom?!

(Sothy walks into the room.)

Sothy: Over here, what happened?

(Buly sees his wife, dashes to her, looks at her, grabs her cheeks, and hugs her close to his heart.)

Buly: I'm sorry. I'll never leave you again as long as you accept me.

Sothy: I waited so long for these words.

(Buly has an idea and gathers the family together in the living room.)

Buly: Let me tell you guys. About me and your mom back in da day. When we fell in love . . .

Danny: Eww *(Somaly smacks his head).*

134   *Modern Literature of Cambodia*

Somaly: Finally! I've been waiting to hear **the unraveling truth** about the love that made me! EEEK! *(Acting super giddy and excited about love)* So much more exciting than a K-drama.

Family: *(In unison)* Shhh! Quiet!

Sorany: Go on, Dad!

Narrator: *(Offstage, speaking as they act out his words.)* The vision that Buly perceived caused him to appreciate what life had given him. He was reminded of how Sothy and he brought life to each other, as well as to their three amazing children. No family is ever perfect. With each other's love and support, no challenge can break a family's bond. As Buly is telling the story of how he and Sothy came to be a couple, Sorany, Somaly, and Danny finally have the family and love they hoped for.

(Curtain slowly closes as the lights dim out.)

THE END

About the Editor

Teri Shaffer Yamada received a master's degree in Southeast Asian languages and literatures in 1975 and a doctorate in Buddhist Studies from the University of California, Berkeley, in 1985. She has studied seven Asian languages, including Chinese, Japanese and Khmer, and lived in Japan for six years. In 2002 she organized the Nou Hach Literary Association (www.nouhachjournal.net) to promote the development of literacy and modern literature in Cambodia. This NGO publishes the only literary journal in Cambodia, sponsors yearly literary awards, and promotes writers workshops in Cambodia. Currently she is the Chair of the Department of Asian and Asian American Studies at CSU Long Beach. Her research interests encompass the areas of modernity and Southeast Asian literature, development and sustainability in Cambodia. Her publications include the compilation *Virtual Lotus: Modern Fiction of Southeast Asia* (Ann Arbor: University of Michigan Press, 2002), *Modern Short Fiction of Southeast Asia: A Literary History* (Ann Arbor: Association for Asian Studies, 2009), and *'Just a Human Being' and Other Tales from Contemporary Cambodia* (Nou Hach Literary Association: Translation Series, No 1, Charleston S.C., 2013). She has written numerous articles on modern Southeast Asian literature and political culture, modern Cambodian literature and culture, and the Cambodian diaspora.

Made in the USA
Middletown, DE
27 November 2022

16132625R00086